W9-DGJ-795

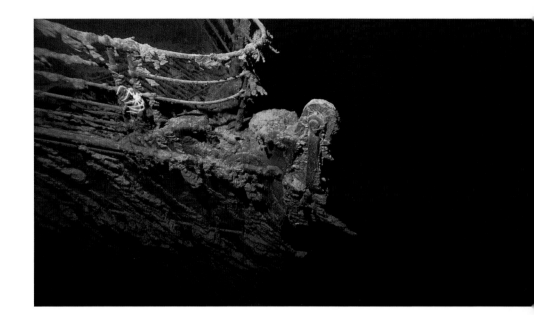

"The story has something for everyone.
For nautical enthusiasts, it is the ultimate shipwreck.
For moralists, there are all those sermons
on overconfidence and self-sacrifice.
For mystics, the omens are irresistible ..."

Walter Lord, *The Night Lives On*

TITANIC

THE LAST GREAT IMAGES

DR. ROBERT BALLARD

WITH IAN COUTTS

RUNNING PRESS
PHILADELPHIA · LONDON

A RUNNING PRESS/MADISON PRESS BOOK

First published in the United States in 2008 by Running Press Book Publishers
All rights reserved under the Pan-American and International Copyright Conventions.

Printed and bound in China

9 8 7 6 5 4 3 2 1
Digit on the right indicates the number of this printing

Library of Congress Control Number: 2007941946

ISBN 978-0-7624-3504-3

Produced by
Madison Press Books
1000 Yonge Street, Suite 200
Toronto, Ontario, Canada
M4W 2K2

This book may be ordered by mail from the publisher. Please include $2.50 for postage and handling. *But try your bookstore first!*

Running Press Book Publishers
2300 Chestnut Street
Philadelphia, PA 19103-4371

Visit us on the web!
www.runningpress.com

Page 1: *Titanic*'s bow.
Pages 2–3: Opening for the number one funnel.
Pages 6–7: The remotely operated vehicle *Hercules* closes in on *Titanic*'s stern.
Pages 8–9: *Titanic*'s mainmast in the ruined stern section.

Contents

A TITANIC DREAM

SEEING *TITANIC* AGAIN was like visiting an old friend.

That was the first thought that flashed through my mind as the initial high-definition images flashed on the large screens in our control van aboard the *Ronald H. Brown*, our research ship from the National Oceanic and Atmospheric Administration. That and how peaceful she looked.

I had returned to *Titanic* in partnership with the National Oceanic and Atmospheric Administration, or NOAA, in April 2004, to demonstrate the very latest in what I long ago dubbed telepresence technology — the use of television cameras and remotely operated vehicles to investigate the deep ocean in real time from the surface. And what better place to demonstrate it than here, on the most famous wreck in history? My first *Titanic* expeditions took place when this technology had been in its earliest stages. We had the dream then (in fact, back in 1981, *National Geographic* published artwork outlining my ideas for the *Argo/Jason* underwater exploration system), but in 1985 we were just starting to realize it. We still had to physically go down to the wreck. My latest trip to *Titanic* was to show the world that the dream had arrived. We were going to bring up the cleanest, clearest images yet of the ship, all shot in high-definition video.

In my control van aboard the research ship *Ronald H. Brown*. I returned to *Titanic* in April 2004, to test out my latest underwater technology, and to see what had happened to the ship in the nearly two decades I had been away.

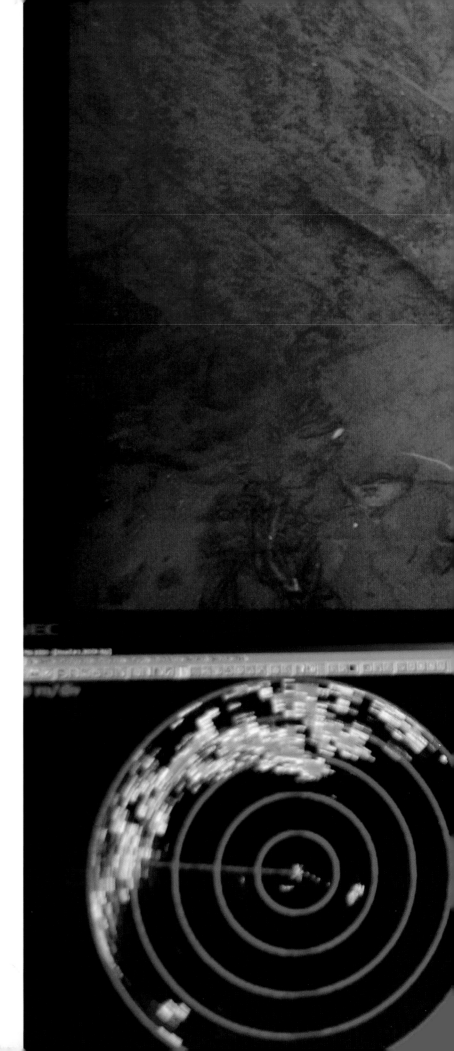

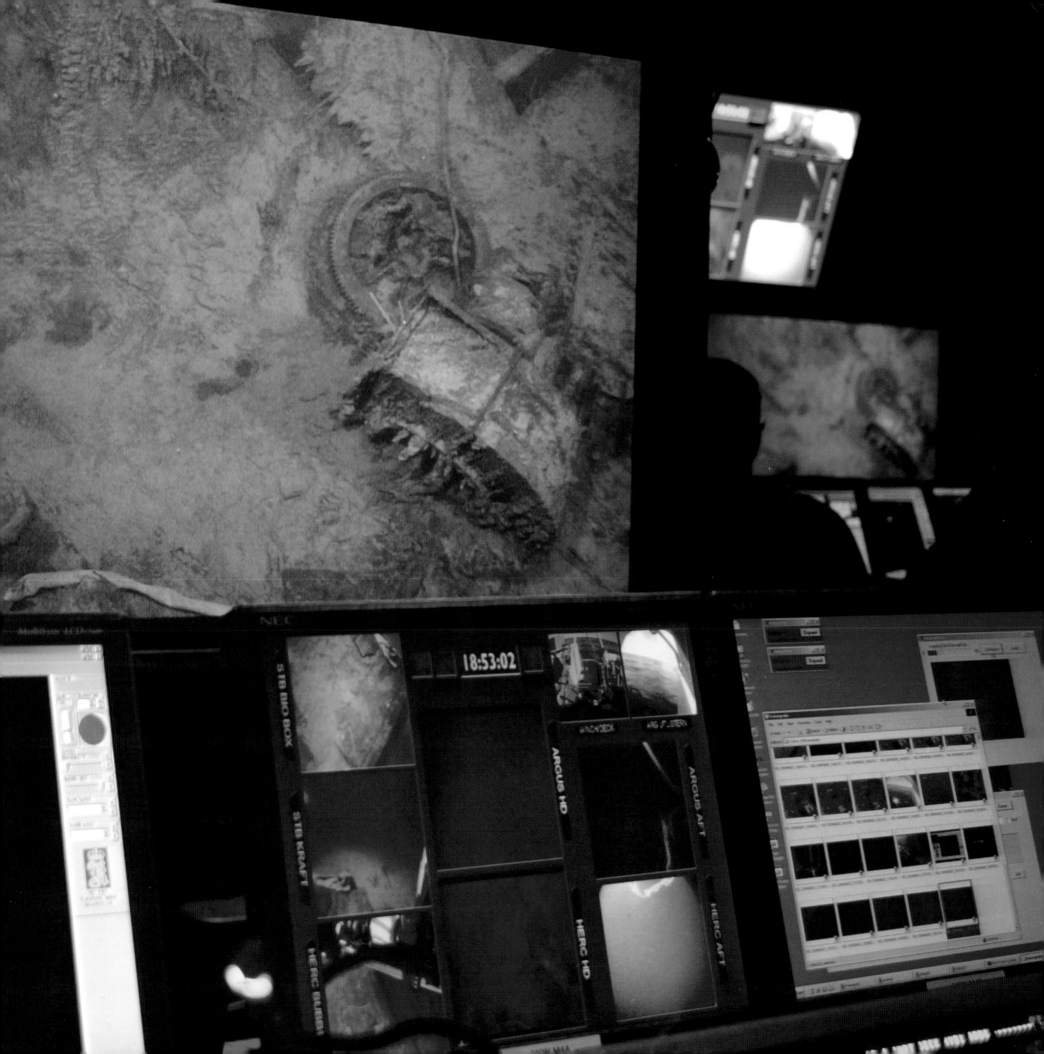

Left: Looking at *Titanic* you quickly see that the extreme end of the bow (where a small submersible cannot put down) is not much changed from twenty years ago.
Right: Other parts of the ship have changed for the worse, like this hole on the starboard side, which is much bigger than when we first visited the ship.
Opposite: *Titanic*'s port anchor swathed in rusticles. The process of decay is always going on, but over time it should slow down, not speed up.

I tell people that I find *Titanic* interesting, but I'm not a James Cameron or a Ken Marschall, who has done so many fantastic paintings of the ship over the years. I don't go to bed at night and dream of it. My first goal, always, has been exploration, never a particular ship. That said, when it comes to *Titanic*, I feel a sense of responsibility. I suppose it's like discovering any historical or archeological site: it's not yours, it's owned by the human race, but one worries about it, one tries to protect it, and one does everything one can for it.

So much has happened since saying goodbye to *Titanic* back in 1986. Those cruises in 1985 and 1986 were so hectic, so unbelievably wrenching. We didn't know if we were going to find the ship, and when we did, everything happened so quickly. Then there were all of the misunderstandings with our French partners and our falling out. After that, I had plenty of other things to keep me busy, but to sit by for twenty years and watch everyone have their way with *Titanic* — often doing things I wasn't terribly happy about — was hard. So I also saw this as an opportunity to pay my respects to the ship, somewhat apologizing for the mean-spirited way in which the wreck has been picked over and vandalized.

The big news before our 2004 expedition to *Titanic* was that the ship seemed to be falling apart far faster than people had originally thought. One of our tasks on this expedition was to take microbial samples for Don Cullimore at the University of Saskatchewan. Cullimore has been investigating the rate of decay of *Titanic*'s metal structure since 1996, and from these numerous experiments he concluded that the ship may well be gone — or at least unrecognizable — in another hundred years or so.

This is distressing news, but I take it with a grain of salt. My sense is that the ship is not decaying as fast as people fear and that we can do things to help preserve it. That was one of our goals. After visiting *Titanic*, we created a mosaic of the ship with the pictures we took, and if you look at the mosaic, you notice something very interesting: where people can't land submarines, there is no damage. In the favorite landing spots up on the bow, right forward of the mast, you can see these obvious, oval-shaped, orange rust patches, marking where submarines have landed. Railings have been carelessly knocked down, too. But look further up in the bow where they can't land, and the deck isn't damaged. It's the same story elsewhere: the captain's cabin, around the grand staircase, over the top of the Marconi Room — anywhere where people and submarines have been poking around — there are holes and other damage. But look down in the well deck, and there's no big change. Why? Because no one goes down there — it's too dangerous. It's the same thing with the stern section of the ship. We collected a complete digital database of the stern and, I must say, since the stern is of no interest to anybody, I see no new damage.

The good news is that *Titanic*'s bow is deeply buried in the mud. Ships are designed to sit that way, and because it is so deeply buried, the mud is holding the whole forward part of the wreck together. If you look at most other ships that are lying on their sides, the *Lusitania* and the *Andrea Doria*, for instance, they are collapsing because they aren't structurally designed to hold themselves that way. The anoxic (that is, oxygen-free) mud is also protecting the hull of *Titanic* from further deterioration.

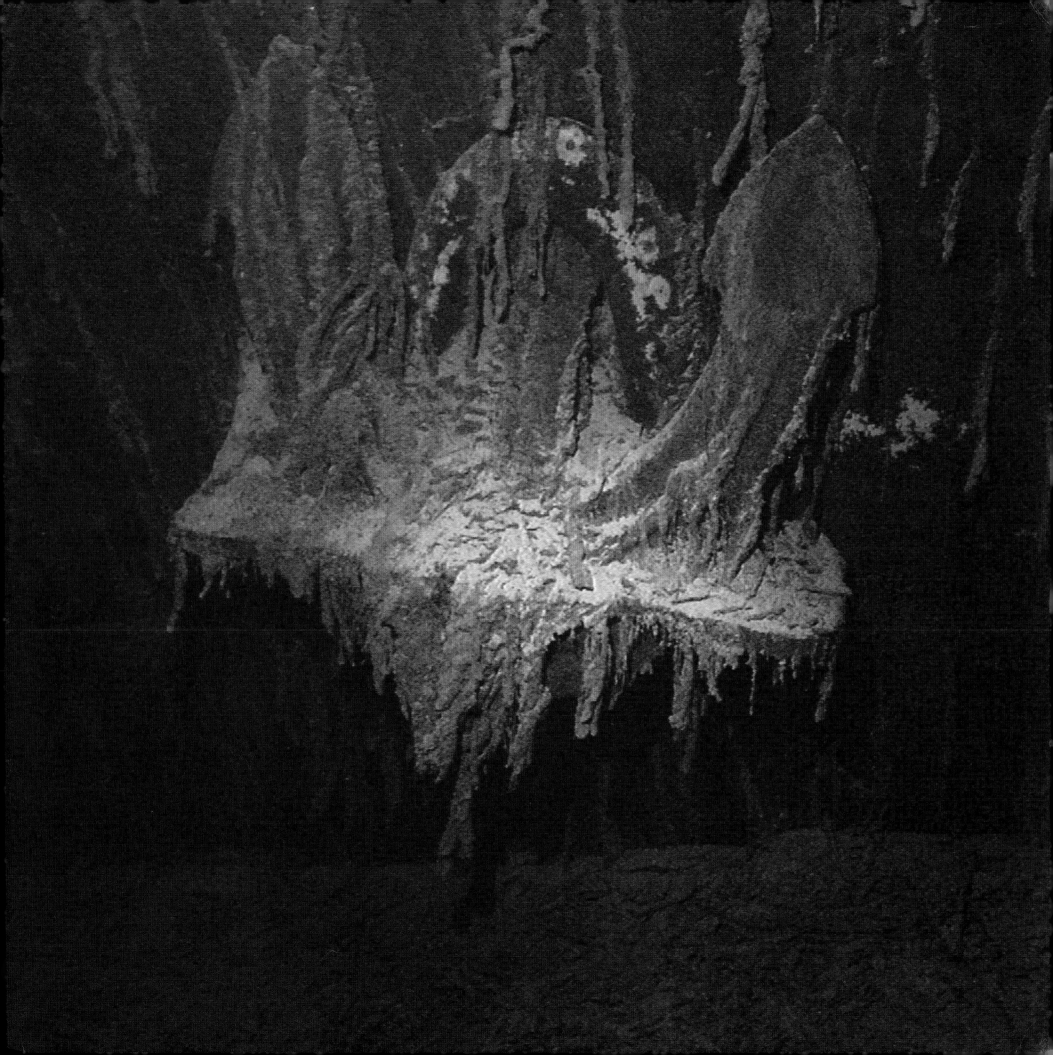

On this trip, I went around the end of the forward section and looked at it closely. I got a better feel for it this time because I could get more adventurous with my robot. All those decks that collapsed on top of each other back here are sitting on the boilers. The boilers are actually holding up the back portion, and with the bow buried, it is in a good situation to be there a long time, as long as visitors don't smash down all of the upper superstructure.

That is the key. Preserving *Titanic* means keeping people away from landing on her. The mauling she has received is not right. I was at Monticello, Thomas Jefferson's great home, recently. That house has been preserved, and it's treated with respect. That's the model for how we should treat *Titanic*. Sure, Monticello is a house on land, but being underwater doesn't change things. Look at the wreck of the *Arizona* at Pearl Harbor, President Jack Kennedy's old command *PT109*, the ships we dived on at Guadalcanal, or the USS *Yorktown* near Midway. Every one of these ships is respected and left alone. Why are ships lost in war treated with respect while the victim of a peacetime tragedy isn't?

In the short run, though, I think that the worst of the mauling may be over. In many ways the salvagers and all the people going out on tour dives are hitting diminishing returns. There haven't been any subsequent expeditions to the ship since our trip there in 2004 (as far as I know, just James Cameron's visit the same year), but more protection is needed. For the past few years, NOAA has been involved in drafting an international treaty that will protect the ship. Dan Basta at NOAA has been working on this and recently told me that it's moving forward and looks really good.

Previous page: Forward on *Titanic*. In various places on the ship we found that railings that used to be upright had been knocked flat by submersibles landing on the decks. Right: We photographed this open stateroom window in 1986. Some things are still the same.

If we can keep people from damaging the ship, then I believe we can proceed with the work of creating a true underwater museum. Look at the wreck now, and what is interesting is that the original anti-fouling paint is still visible on the hull. When we came in on the starboard side the first time, back in 1986, I thought, "My God, the paint's still there." It was still there in 2004, still doing its job. The technology exists to clean and paint *Titanic* in place, halting the decay.

We could then place cameras and remotely operated vehicles inside, and you'd be able to visit it via telepresence, go right inside the ship and see what's there.

What we are talking about, ultimately, is electronic travel — the day when Hertz will rent robots so we can visit the Serengeti remotely, or even a great liner at the bottom of the sea. This isn't science fiction. We're implementing it in other places. Obviously it will be a while before we jump to 12,500 feet, but we are installing cameras and ROVs in marine sanctuaries right now, and operating them remotely. And we're now coming up with new imaging technologies that will make it feel like really being there. The underwater cables that have been going around *Titanic* for more than a hundred years can be tapped into to relay the images back to land.

I know we can implement this dream. Is it a decade away? Maybe. But in the meantime there is another record of the *Titanic*, here in these pages, featuring the most recent images of the great wreck and what I am sure are the clearest and most vivid ever taken. We won't have another chance to see the ship this closely again for at least ten years. That is, if the dream comes true.

Opposite: Exploring *Titanic* via our control room monitors.

Top, left to right: Launching the remotely operated vehicle *Hercules* from the research ship *Ronald H. Brown. Hercules'* digital cameras have produced the clearest most detailed pictures of *Titanic* ever.
Above: The deterioration of the ship is especially visible here.

Overleaf: The square ports of the promenade deck can just be made out in this picture. How much will still be recognizable in a few years, on the 100th anniversary of the sinking?

CHAPTER ONE

Dead Ships Do Tell Tales

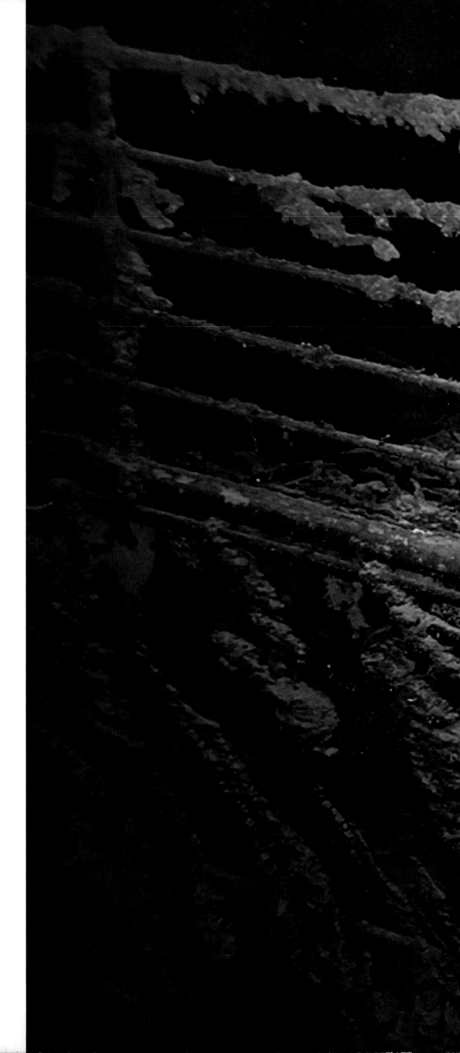

She sits today 12,500 feet below the surface, in waters that hover near freezing in temperature and in perpetual darkness. Broken in two, *Titanic* is rusty and badly battered, but still, for all that, recognizably a passenger ship, a great passenger ship of the Edwardian era. For more than seventy years she slumbered on the bottom undisturbed, until my team and I found her on September 1, 1985.

This we know. But when it comes to *Titanic*, it is never easy to separate the legend from the facts, to get away from the mythic story and see what really happened. Today, we often see her only as a metaphor for man's hubris, a fantastic tragedy set aboard the world's most luxurious, arrogant creation.

The broad strokes of the story are simple enough to outline. She was, at the time of her launch, the largest ship in the world, 882.9 feet long and with a displacement of more than 53,000 tons. She left Southampton, on England's south coast, on Wednesday, April 10, 1912, on her maiden voyage to New York. She never made it. Four days later, on the evening of Sunday, April 14, 1912, she hit an iceberg and sank early the next morning, with the loss of more than fifteen hundred lives.

But, right from the start, the *Titanic* story has been about more than the broad strokes. There has always been another dimension. Giving a ship a name like *Titanic* in the first place was an act of pride, if there ever was one. Then there was the claim that she was unsinkable. True, the White Star Line, the ship's owners, never said that. The closest anyone ever came to making such a

Right: *Titanic*'s bow today. The ship may be rusty and battered, but the wreck today is still recognizable as a great liner of the Edwardian time. What appear to be plants growing on the railings are actually marine animals — no vegetable life can survive at these sunless depths.

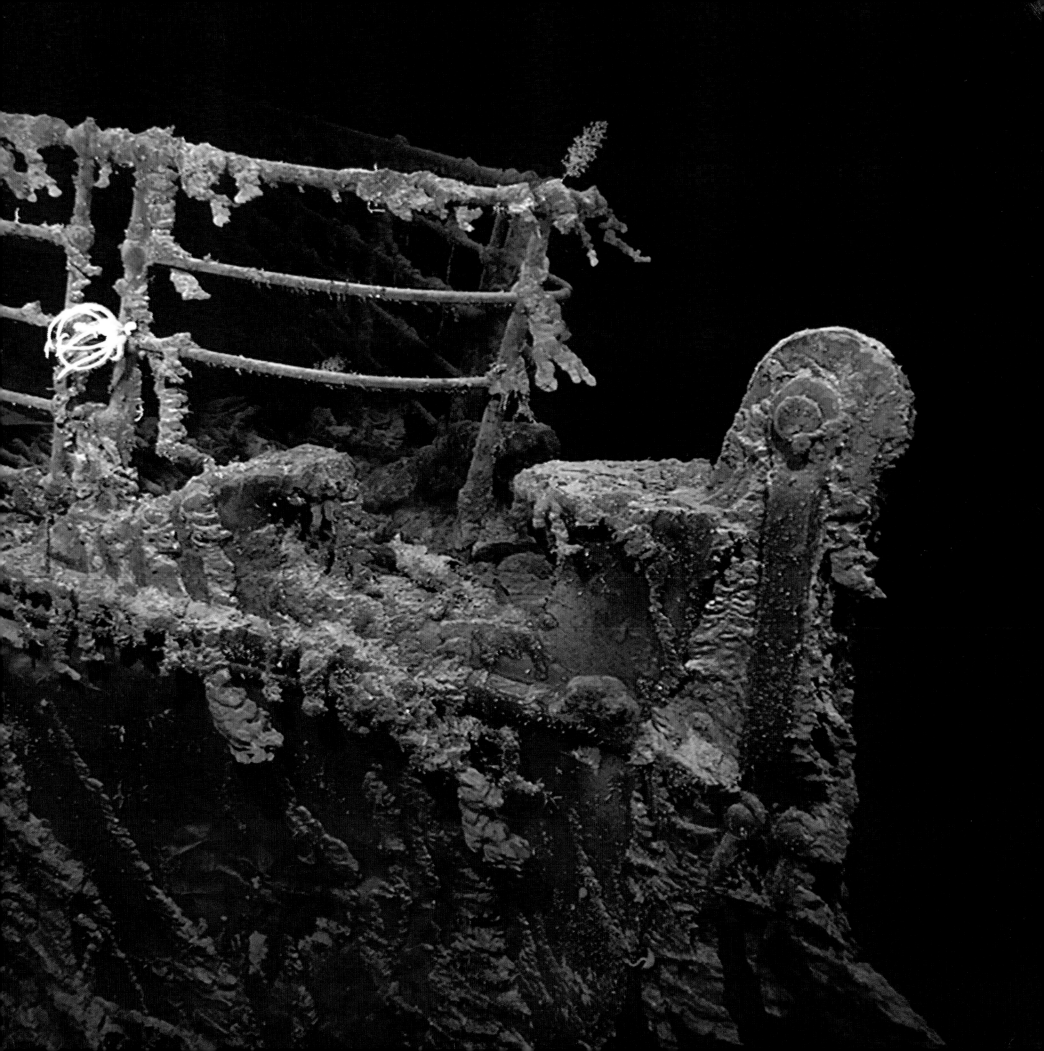

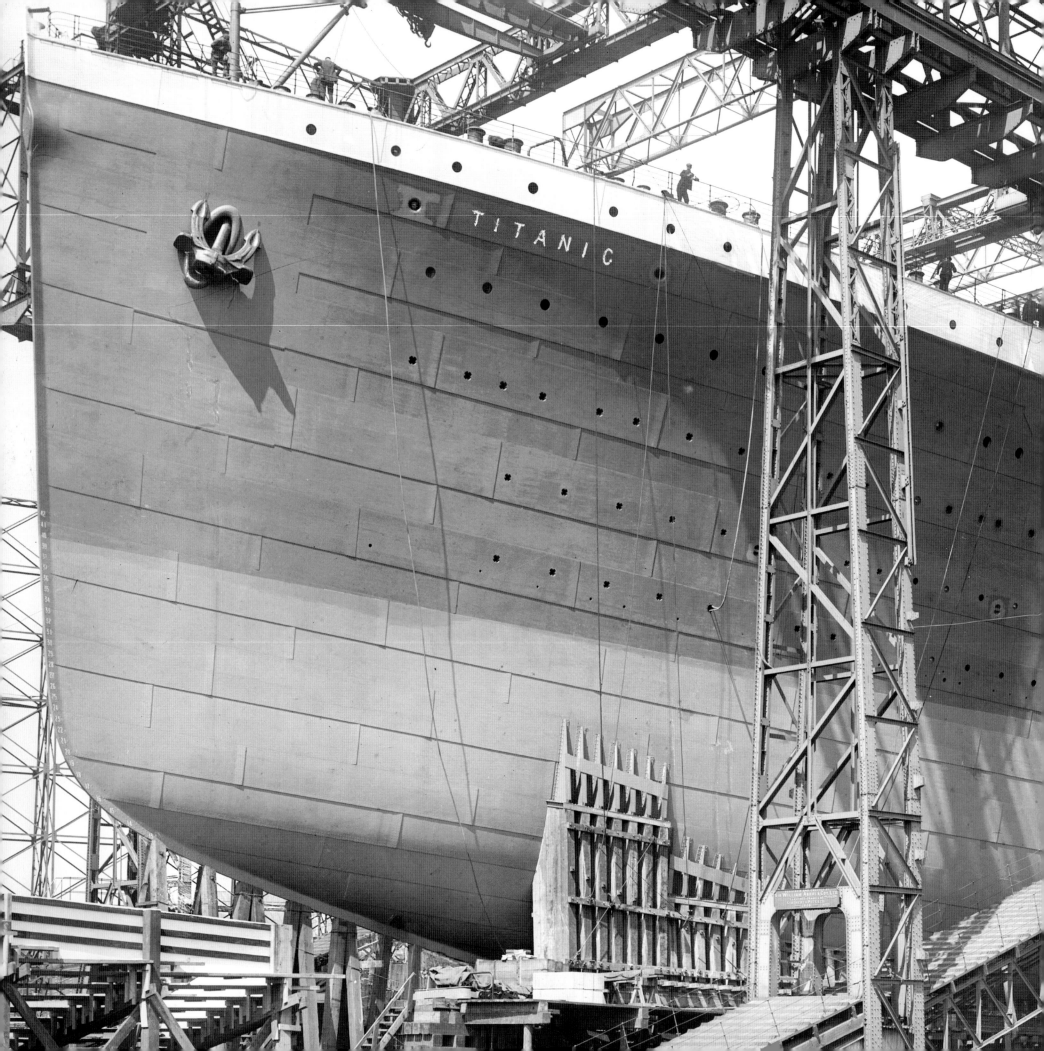

Left: *Titanic* under construction at the Harland and Wolff yard in Belfast. To build *Titanic* and her sister *Olympic*, Harland and Wolff had to build the world's largest gantry, which can be seen here over the ship.

claim was a British trade magazine, *The Shipbuilder*, which asserted in an article on the new liner that her watertight compartments and other safety features made her "practically unsinkable." Somewhere along the line that key adverb got dropped, and everyone started telling each other that nothing could send the new liner to the bottom.

Any ship's maiden voyage is a noteworthy event, but there were few that could match *Titanic*'s. Many of the most prominent members of the era's transatlantic plutocracy booked passage — John Jacob Astor, Benjamin Guggenheim, and the Denver mining millionairess Mrs. J.J. Brown. These were people whose comings and goings were followed avidly in the popular press, and they all wanted to travel on the newest and most luxurious ship afloat, under the steady hand of Edward Smith, White Star's famed "millionaire's captain." A classic, gray-bearded British sea dog, this was to be Smith's farewell voyage after decades of distinguished service; once he had seen the new liner across the ocean and home again, he planned to retire. Nor should we forget J. Bruce Ismay, the director of the White Star Line, who was also sailing on that maiden voyage. Some say that the completion of *Titanic* was his final victory in a life-long struggle to emerge from his father's shadow.

Looking back, the ship's first sailing seems to have been saddled with more than its share of dramatic foreshadowing. There were the premonitions of those who chose not to sail at the very last moment. The uncanny fact that fourteen years earlier the American author Morgan Robertson had penned a novel called *Futility*, in which a grand ocean liner hits an iceberg on her maiden voyage.

Opposite: Her name clearly visible on her bow, *Titanic* stands ready for launching. Sliding the ship into the water would require 23 tons of tallow, train oil, and soft soap.

Above: *Titanic* hits the water, Wednesday, May 31, 1911. Thousands of spectators watched the event, many seated in grandstands built for the occasion. Overleaf: *Titanic* leaves the docks in Southampton on her maiden voyage, April 10, 1912.

The name of Robertson's doomed ship? *Titan*. And rumor had it that there was an Egyptian mummy, complete with inevitable curse, down in the cargo hold. (It was only a rumor.)

At every point, the *Titanic* story seems to unfold with an eye for the dramatic. On the evening of April 14, had the iceberg been spotted but a few moments earlier, the ship would have been able to turn enough to miss it; once the iceberg was spotted, had the on-duty officer on the bridge not ordered the engines reversed, the ship might still have glided safely past the frozen menace. Indeed, if *Titanic* had simply plowed headlong into the iceberg, she would have been better off, likely limping into New York a few days later than expected, perhaps under tow from another ship. That would have been a humiliating end to a maiden voyage, but over the subsequent decades of her career, it would have been forgotten — as *Titanic* herself would ultimately have been, by all but a few liner buffs. But no, *Titanic* struck the iceberg, just so, opening a long wound in her side that meant that six of her watertight compartments were ruptured. The ship had been designed to float with four of the forward compartments flooded; six was fatal. (Some *Titanic* buffs speculate that, had First Officer William Murdoch not acted so quickly to slam the doors connecting the ship's watertight compartments, *Titanic* would have filled more evenly and much more slowly, perhaps allowing time for help to arrive on the scene.)

The ship's wireless operators got busy, using the new SOS distress call, another first. The nearest ship they could raise — the Cunard liner *Carpathia* — was several hours away. *Titanic* carried fourteen regulation lifeboats, two slightly smaller sea boats, and four collapsible boats intended to be launched after the regular boats had been lowered. All perfectly according to regulation, better in fact than what Britain's Board of Trade required, but still only enough for about half the people aboard that night. The great ship took roughly two and a half hours to sink, plenty of time for a range of human stories and emotions to be played out — disbelief and panic, courage and cowardice, even real nobility.

"BE BRITISH" : The Last Words of the "Titanic's" Captain.

Left: For Captain Edward Smith, *Titanic*'s maiden voyage was to be his last command before retiring. Below: Smith orders the wireless operator to send the distress call.

The "S-O-S"

Titanic's sinking was, in its day, as profound a tragedy as could be imagined. But perhaps because in a little over two years the world was embroiled in the Great War, after the initial shock and a relative flurry of books, the world turned away from *Titanic*.

The ship may have been out of sight, but she was never really out of mind, if only on a subconscious level. Slowly, over the decades, *Titanic* the ship began to give way to *Titanic* the legend. In 1955, Walter Lord published his classic study of the sinking, *A Night to Remember*. As strange as it seems to us, given how big a place *Titanic* holds in the public consciousness, his was the first book written on the ship in more than four decades. Lord's telling was particularly effective because he managed to collar many of the then-elderly survivors just at the point where they were beginning to exit the stage. *A Night to Remember* was a bestseller, and later a popular movie. Ever since, *Titanic*'s mythic status has kept growing. Our discovery of the ship stoked people's interest even more. Already the most famous maritime disaster, for a second act, *Titanic* then clinched a new title, that of world's most famous wreck.

James Cameron's 1997 epic, *Titanic,* was the final stage in the creation of the ship's legend, a rip-roaring, adventure-romance featuring an incredibly accurate recreation of the ship and its sinking. The film became, when released, the highest-grossing movie of all time. Since then, new books and articles, further expeditions to the wreck, traveling shows, and additional films have all kept *Titanic* in the public eye. The great, doomed liner really does seem to be, as Walter Lord put it in his follow-up to *A Night to Remember*, "the unsinkable subject." The *Titanic* mythology has achieved some sort of critical mass, and it sometimes feels as if it could feed on itself forever, each retelling generating further versions of the story.

Still, time marches on, and the actual tragedy is growing ever more distant. At the time of writing, there is but one survivor left alive, Elizabeth Gladys "Millivina" Dean. Predeceased by Barbara Joyce Dainton West on October 16, 2007, both were babes in arms on the night of the sinking. The last survivor who could actually

Opposite: Popular depictions like this one filled the illustrated magazines at the time of the *Titanic* disaster. The fate of the "unsinkable" liner shocked people, but when war broke out in 1914, the sinking was forgotten.

The 1955 publication of Walter Lord's *A Night to Remember*, followed by the release of the movie version three years later (left), revived interest in the ship. Below: Fascination with the doomed liner hit a new high with the 1997 release of *Titanic*, directed by James Cameron, pictured here on set.

remember the events of April 14, 1912, Lillian Gertrud Asplund, died in May 2006, aged ninety-nine. If we want to try for a more direct, physical contact with the "night to remember," we can, if we so choose, take in one of the touring shows featuring items salvaged (some would say pillaged) from *Titanic*. But it's not really the same. These souvenirs have been stripped from their context, and few of those objects are truly specific to the ship. One teacup bearing the logo of the White Star Line is very much like another.

What we do have is the wreck itself. Dead men, the old cliché has it, tell no tales. Dead ships, however, do. Look at a wreck the right way and it will tell you stories. Stories about the glory days of transatlantic voyaging, the triumph of Edwardian technology, or an ordered social world where everyone had a place, knew it, and knew how they were expected to behave. Stories about a night of tragedy and terror and real heroism, about the search to find this greatest of all lost ships. We can see where lookout Frederick Fleet was when he spotted the iceberg, stand where Captain Smith stood when he understood that the ship was lost and, yes, we can even see the spot where Kate Winslett's Rose DeWitt Bukater character spread her arms and imagined she was flying on the bow of the ship.

I have talked about my hope that some day *Titanic* will be a true underwater museum, one which, thanks to the installation of cameras throughout the wreck, people would be able to tour by logging on to a site on their computers whenever they felt like it. We don't need to wait for that future day. Thanks to our 2004 expedition, we have clear, large-scale photographs of the wreck that

let us look at her in a way that has not been possible before; that help us to think about the ship as not just a wreck, but as an enormous collection of artifacts, like a battlefield left untouched after the firing has ceased, or the ancient city of Pompeii. Here, the world remains frozen as it was over ninety-five years ago. Here, we can, in this grim tomb, strip away the legend and return to the original stories of *Titanic*. For that is what the *Titanic* is, not one story, but many, each one overlaying the other, like the layers of silt on the deep ocean floor.

The stories are there, waiting for us. All we need to do is look.

A photo mosaic showing *Titanic* as it looked when Robert Ballard found it in 1985, created from pictures taken on that expedition.

Previous page: The remains of *Titanic*'s bridge seen in high-definition video in the control van aboard the **NOAA** ship, *Ronald H. Brown*.

Right: *Hercules*, one of our **ROV**s, leaves test materials on the ship's deck to gauge the rate of *Titanic*'s decay.
Below: *Titanic*'s forecastle deck, a popular landing spot for submersibles. The orange patches are signs of recent damage.

Left: A ship's port hole festooned with rusticles, which are created by iron-eating bacteria. Over time, if *Titanic* were left alone, they would consume it entirely — but at a much slower rate than it is currently disappearing.

Right: This skylight, on the port side of the forecastle just before the well deck, provided natural light for the crew's quarters.
Overleaf: The same skylight visible above can be seen here in the upper left hand of this picture, looking forward from *Titanic*'s well deck.

CHAPTER TWO

THE TECHNICAL MARVEL

WITH ITS DOMED TOP and that row of large, circling bolts, it looks a bit like an old-fashioned fire hydrant. It seems to recede into the darkness and, if you look off, a second circle is just visible. But it seems almost impossible to get a sense of scale.

In fact, this is the head for one of the cylinders in the ship's two enormous reciprocating engines, cylinders that stand forty feet from this tip to their base. Each engine boasted four such cylinders of varying diameters, each encasing an enormous piston attached to a propeller shaft. They operated in a fashion similar to the pistons in a car engine. Super-heated steam was first fed into a high-pressure cylinder pushing it down; from there, the steam, now slightly cooler and under less pressure, fed into a second cylinder, starting it moving, then into a third and finally a fourth.

Titanic's powerful, twin triple-expansion reciprocating engines were, at the time, the largest of their kind in the world. Each produced a total of 15,000 horsepower and could turn a ship's propeller at up to 75 revolutions per minute.

However powerful, they were by no means the latest word in technology. Reciprocating engines like *Titanic*'s were essentially the same as the original steam engine that James Watt had invented more than one hundred years before, albeit much improved examples. By the early twentieth century, thanks to the work of the British inventor Charles Parsons, a new kind of engine, the steam turbine, was taking its place. Equipped with a large number of enclosed blades mounted on a central shaft, the steam turbine used

One of the high-pressure cylinders from *Titanic*'s starboard reciprocating engines. Four stories in height, they were the largest engines of their kind in the world. This cylinder sits exposed in the wreckage of the stern section, just aft of where the ship broke in two before sinking.

Right: Sir Charles Parson's revolutionary ship *Turbinia*, which he built to show off his high-speed steam turbines.
Below: One of *Titanic's* reciprocating engines before installation in the ship.

high-pressure steam in much the same way that a windmill might depend upon a stiff breeze. The result was a powerful means of propulsion that was also much smaller and more efficient than any reciprocating engine. Parsons had illustrated his turbine's effectiveness at the 1897 Spithead Naval Review, held to celebrate Queen Victoria's sixtieth anniversary on the throne. Onlookers had been astonished as Parson's experimental ship, *Turbinia*, dashed in and around the anchored battleships, before easily outrunning the fast torpedo boats sent to catch her. From then on, the turbine found fast acceptance. The Cunard Line's *Carmania,* launched in 1905, was equipped with them, as was the Royal Navy's revolutionary battleship *Dreadnought*, also launched that year.

In fact, *Titanic* did boast one turbine engine, which powered the central of the ship's three propellers. The engine was the result of an experiment by Harvard and Wolff using a combination of reciprocating and turbine engines. This was an unusual setup, one which simultaneously embraced the very latest technology, while holding on to what was tried and true. To understand White Star's use of this dual setup, you need to understand the competitive climate on the North Atlantic and the role that *Titanic* — and by extension the ship's owners, the White Star Line — played in it.

The White Star Line had originally been founded to run adventurers and supplies from England to Australia at the height of that nation's gold rush. Bankrupt in the late 1860s, in 1869 a new company, Oceanic Steam Navigation Company, under the helm of T. H. Ismay, bought the White Star name, flag, and goodwill. The Australian run had been all right, but that was not where the money was to be made. That was on the North Atlantic. Between the years 1840 and 1890, transatlantic trade increased incredibly, sevenfold in cotton, tobacco, and wheat alone. Perhaps even more important was the rapid increase in the population of the United States. People from all over Europe were looking to make a new life in America, and there was money to be made carrying them there. There was a smattering of people who were willing to pay dearly for a transatlantic trip, but the bulk of the trade was in "steerage" passengers, so-called because their accommodation was found low in the ship's stern, near the steering gear.

Even by the time that White Star entered the transatlantic business, however, a single company already dominated the traffic between the United States and Great Britain. This was the famed Cunard Line, founded by Nova Scotia native Samuel Cunard in 1840. Originally, Cunard had concentrated mostly on its lucrative contract to move mail across the Atlantic, carrying just a few passengers, none of them in steerage. Sailing on fixed schedules — an innovation made possible thanks to the advent of steam powered ships, eliminating the need to wait for favorable winds — Cunard quickly established a reputation for safety and speed. After fending off an assault on their dominant position by the American-owned Collins Line in the 1850s (Collins' ships had a tendency to sink, often with great loss of life, a fact that quickly doomed the line), Cunard had emerged as the leader on the Atlantic a little after the mid-century mark.

For most of the second half of the nineteenth century, Great Britain dominated the North Atlantic run, thanks to Cunard, White Star and, to a lesser extent, Liverpool's Inman Line, with the cut-throat competition leading to amazing advances in ship-building. Passenger liners began to lose their resemblance to sailing ships: the yardarms grew ever smaller, and White Star's *Teutonic,* launched in 1889, was the first ship to do away with sails altogether. The raked clipper bows of yore gave way to blunter bows, which reflected the shift in building materials from wood to iron and then to steel. Ships grew larger and faster, and considerably more comfortable. White Star's *Oceanic (1)*, beginning service in 1871, had been the first ship to move the first-class accommodation from the stern forward to midships, where the vibrations from the ship's screws were milder. The traditionally cramped dining saloons were opened up, at least for the high-paying passengers, and the food served improved considerably as well.

Left: Originally from Nova Scotia, Samuel Cunard revolutionized the transatlantic shipping business and his line dominated the trade for much of the nineteenth century.

Below: The White Star Line's *Teutonic*. She was the first liner built with twin screws and without yards to carry sails, a major advance.

Right: Cunard's *Lusitania* and *Mauretania* pass each other on Liverpool's River Mersey.
Below: *Mauretania*'s first-class dining room was done up in dark woods suggestive of an English country house.

Competition intensified in the 1890s when German lines, eager to slice off a share of the big money to be made on these routes, began building the gigantic new liners. The Inman Line was bought in 1893 by the American Line, and then in 1902, the American tycoon J. P. Morgan bought White Star, adding it to his International Mercantile Marine Company (J. Bruce Ismay, son of White Star's founder, became president of the IMMC in 1904). Morgan's dream was to create a monopoly on North Atlantic shipping, eliminating competition and standardizing costs of travel. This prompted a price war among the major companies, and, at one point, fares from Europe to the U.S. were as low as two pounds.

In 1907, the Cunard steamship line launched two ships that re-asserted its dominance, while taking the battle for supremacy to a new level. *Lusitania* and *Mauretania*, built by the great shipyards John Brown and Co. and Swann Hunter, respectively, were big (*Lusitania* was 785 feet long, sister *Mauretania*, 780) and beautifully decorated. *Lusitania* was done up in a fashion that recalled the styles of the Georgian era and Louis XVI opulence, all white paneling and gold leaf, while *Mauretania* favored a look that was more English baronial, heavy on the carved oak and mahogany. Above all, they were *fast*. The chairman of Cunard had managed to squeeze money out of the British government to pay for their construction. The money was in part to make sure that Cunard did not fall into foreign hands, but also with the idea that the ships could be designed so that they might be converted to armed merchant cruisers in wartime. Under the agreement between Cunard and the British government, this meant a designed maximum speed of 24.5 knots. In fact, both ships easily exceeded this. *Lusitania* made 26 knots on her trials, *Mauretania* a shade more. *Lusitania* snagged the mythic "blue riband," the accolade granted to the fastest ship on an Atlantic crossing, not long after she entered regular service. Soon "Lucy" and her sister "Maury" were passing the riband back and forth from one voyage to the next.

Even before *Lusitania* had made her maiden voyage, White Star was planning its next move in the race to stay ahead on the North Atlantic. Legend has it that in the summer of 1907, the director of the International Marine and White Star, J. Bruce Ismay, and his wife went to dinner at Downshire House, the London home of the Right Honorable Lord and Lady Pirrie. Pirrie was a director of the Belfast shipbuilders Harland and Wolff, who built nearly all of the White Star ships.

Ismay did not want to see Cunard get the upper hand, and Pirrie cannot have wanted to see White Star, one of Harland and Wolff's biggest customers, squeezed out of the North Atlantic trade. Together that evening, so the story goes, they hatched a plan to do Cunard one better: they would build two great ships, with a third to follow, that would be bigger than the two new Cunarders. Each would displace fifty percent more than the *Lusitania*'s 30,000 tons and be nearly 100 feet longer, at 882 feet rather than a whisker under 790. They would in fact be the world's biggest liners. Both men agreed from the start that there would be no attempt to match the new Cunarders in terms of speed. Their new super ships would make good speed, rather than great speed, and concentrate instead on comfort for those in steerage and greater luxury for those sailing in first class. This was one reason for the use of large reciprocating engines rather than depending exclusively on the new high-pressure turbines. They could not have known it for certain at this point, but their decision would be a wise one. *Lusitania* and *Mauretania* proved to be fast, certainly, but they were also, as a result, uncomfortable. *Lusitania* had severe vibration problems that required a good deal of structural stiffening to lessen, and they were never quite fixed. Also, the ships' sheer bows and relatively narrow beams, again intended to provide for greater speeds, made for a rough ride in bad weather. Both tended to lunge into oncoming waves rather than ride over them.

Look at the aft end of *Titanic*'s forward section today, and you will see these boilers standing five in a row. Their fronts have been pushed in slightly, thanks to the water pressure on them as the ship sank

Left: Lord and Lady Pirrie standing before their Belfast house. A director of Harland and Wolff, he and the White Star Line's J. Bruce Ismay dreamed up three great liners, including *Titanic*.

Above: Shipyard workers pose behind the center and port propellers of *Titanic*'s sister *Olympic*.

MAIN BOILERS

Previous page: *Titanic* boilers still in place, and holding up the ship's collapsed decks, in the number two boiler room. The deep sea pressure has pushed the boilers' faces in.

Above: *Olympic*'s boilers awaiting installation in a workshop at Harland and Wolff. Each liner boasted twenty-nine boilers, which needed up to 640 tons of coal a day to drive the ships at 21 knots.

Opposite: The two great liners sit side by side under the massive gantry at Harland and Wolff on the day of *Olympic*'s launch, October 20, 1910. *Olympic* began her maiden voyage on June 14, 1911.

The numerous small circles visible on their front are the ends of tubes that held the water that would be turned into steam. Whether a ship was powered by turbines or reciprocating engines, it all came down to the same brute truth: what really propelled *Titanic* were the dozens of stokers who worked in her six boiler rooms, feeding the ship's twenty-nine boilers with coal. That steam drove the world's largest reciprocating engines and the great turbine, which were in turn connected to the ship's three propellers.

Fittingly, for the biggest ship in the world, the propellers were the largest of their kind. Each of the blades alone is taller than a man. All in, the side propellers on *Titanic* were 23 feet across and weighed 38 tons apiece. The center prop was a slightly more modest affair, spanning just 16 ? feet from blade tip to blade tip and weighing 22 tons.

Biggest ship, biggest engines, biggest propellers. Such superlatives are great fun to bandy about, but they represented incredible challenges for the builders of the *Olympic* and *Titanic*. In fact, when Pirrie and Ismay hatched their grandiose dream, Harland and Wolff did not have the means to actually construct the ships. Nor, for that matter, was the White Star pier in New York long enough for the new ships to dock at. And the ship channel in Southampton would have to be dredged out so *Titanic* and her sister *Olympic* could use the port. But these were mere trifles.

While Pirrie's design staff labored to create plans for the two new ships, workmen busily converted what had been three separate slipways in the shipyard into two large frameworks, where the two sisters would be constructed side by side. A 220-foot-tall gantry — in keeping with the grandiose nature of the project, the largest in the world — was built over the slips. Finally, on March 31, 1909, workmen laid the first keel plate for *Titanic*. Work on her sister *Olympic* had started the previous December.

The basic construction of *Titanic*, from the laying of that initial keel plate until she slid down the ways on May 31, 1911, recognizably a ship if still not ready for service, took a little over two years.

Right: Long rows of rivets, rusting but still intact, are visible here.
Opposite: A shot of *Titanic*'s starboard side taken at Queenstown, showing some of the more than three million rivets used in the liner's construction.

Right: This fragment of *Titanic* on the bottom today shows the inside of the hull, notably the steel ribs that the plating was riveted to.

A modern yard could, of course, squeeze out a ship in less time. For example, the British carrier HMS *Ocean*, which was deliberately built using civilian methods of construction to save money and time, took a little more than a year and half from when its keel was laid in May 1994 until it slid down the ways in October 1995. *Ocean* is smaller than *Titanic*, to be sure, but what is almost awe-inspiring about the construction of *Titanic* is how it was built. A modern ship, and this holds for naval vessels to cruise liners, is welded, often by automated equipment guided by computers. But if we look at a section of *Titanic*'s hull, either part of the ship that is intact or a portion that has broken off, we notice that *Titanic* was constructed by riveting together thousands of tons of steel. First the pieces that made up her keel and ribs, and then the many plates that would make up her hull.

The riveting crews worked in groups of four, starting at six in the morning and going till about half past five at night. First, the "heater" heated the rivet in what looked like a brazier, kept going with a foot bellows. When the rivet was glowing red, he picked it up in a set of tongs and tossed it to a "rivet passer," who then stuck the still-hot rivet through a hole in two overlapping plates. A third man, called the "holder-up," held the rivet in place by putting a hammer underneath it, and two men working on the other side of the plate hammered and beat up the point of the rivet, securing it. The crew was estimated to "do about two hundred rivets a day in *Titanic*'s time, provided it didn't rain" (if it did, their pay stopped and they were sent home). This is especially impressive when you consider that *Titanic*'s construction required three million rivets. In the days before the First World War, Harland and Wolff employed 15,000 men, of whom, according to the company, some 3,000 would in May 1911, the month of her launch, have been actively working on *Titanic*. Three million rivets at a rate of 200 a day represents 15,000 days of work for a four-man crew.

We cannot see it today when we look at the wreck on the bottom, but one of the jobs the riveters would have undertaken was the construction of the ship's double bottom. This was precisely what the name implies, a second hull inside the main hull of the ship. The outer hull of the ship was steel at least an inch thick, which sounds thin, but by modern standards is quite substantial and would provide the ship with a fair degree of protection. The inner hull was thinner, but it would, if *Titanic* hit anything well below the waterline that managed to broach the outer hull, protect her from sinking. This was not the only safety feature built into the ship. As a further structural safety feature, the hull of *Titanic* was divided into a series of watertight compartments that extended ten feet above the waterline. Home to the ship's boilers and engines, these compartments were connected by doors that could be closed automatically by throwing a switch on the bridge in case of trouble. Several compartments had to be broached for the ship to sink — more than two amidships or four forward. Once the ship had been launched, and hauled by tugs to the fitting-out basin, further safety features were added: sixteen lifeboats and a powerful new Marconi wireless transmitter.

Any discussion of *Titanic*'s safety features is, it almost goes without saying, one tinged with irony. When we read discussions of the ship's supposed "unsinkability," we attribute people's confidence in her to a misplaced belief in progress or some sort of untrammeled Edwardian hubris. These did play a part in the catastrophe, but the

Top: The gash in
Olympic's side after
HMS *Hawke* hit the liner
off the Isle of Wight, on
September 20, 1911.

Above: Thanks to the
ship's wireless call for
help, after the White Star
liner *Republic* was rammed
off Nantucket on January
23, 1909, vessels raced to
rescue her passengers.

men who designed and built *Titanic* were not fools. A good deal of
their confidence in the ship's ability to survive had, at least, some
basis in fact.

A little over two years before the launch of *Titanic*, the White Star
liner *Republic*, bound for the Mediterranean from New York, was
rammed amidships in fog southwest of Nantucket Island. It quickly
became obvious that *Republic* was doomed. However, thanks to her
twelve watertight compartments, although she was flooding, the ship
was sinking very slowly. As the ship filled, her wireless operator, Jack
Binns, sent off a distress call that was picked up on Nantucket and
immediately relayed to all other ships at sea. After a few hours of
drama, the passengers and crew of *Republic* were evacuated, first by
the ship that rammed them, and then transferred to another ship
called to the scene by wireless. In the end, *Republic* did sink, with the
loss of only three lives, all people killed in the collision. Wireless had
saved the day; the sole function of the ship's lifeboats had been to
shift passengers from the hapless *Republic* to waiting rescuers.

Still, if you had an eye for it, there was a disturbing portent. On
September 20, 1911, while *Titanic* was still fitting-out in Belfast, her
sister *Olympic* was embarking on her fifth voyage to New York since
being accepted by the White Star Line. After leaving Southampton,
Olympic swung east, heading for Cherbourg in France to pick up additional passengers. As she was passing between the mainland and
the north side of the Isle of Wight, a British cruiser, HMS *Hawke*,
was rounding the end of the Isle and steaming west. No one is sure
exactly how it happened, but *Hawke* hit *Olympic*, badly damaging
her own bow and tearing a hole in *Olympic*'s starboard side, after
which the much smaller ship bobbed away, in the words of its com-
mander, "like a cork." The Royal Navy said that *Olympic*'s sheer bulk
created a sort of suction that caused *Hawke*'s steering to jam, draw-
ing the hapless warship into its side. An admiralty court found
Olympic and its captain, Edward Smith, soon to take command of
Titanic, to be at fault. Perhaps these new enormous ships weren't as
nimble or maneuverable as the liners of just a few years earlier.

On February 3, 1912, tugs moved *Titanic* from the fitting-out dock to her final stop before completion, the Belfast Harbour Commission's new graving dock. *Titanic*'s completion had been delayed because *Olympic*'s extensive repairs required that men working on the new ship be pulled from their duties to get the damaged liner seaworthy again. Once the water was pumped out of the dock, *Titanic*'s great propellers were installed and the ship was given a final coat of paint. Sea trials had been scheduled for April 1, but strong winds on that morning had raised concerns about trying to maneuver the ship through the River Lagan and along the Victoria Channel. So it was that the next day *Titanic* dropped her shore lines and, towed by two large tugs, began to make her way out into Belfast Lough. Over the next few hours, under the watchful eyes of representatives from Harland and Wolff, the British Board of Trade (who would certify her seaworthy) and the White Star Line, Captain Smith put the liner through her paces: stopping then restarting the great ship, executing a series of tight turns, and running on only two engines. On leaving Belfast Lough for the waters of the Irish Sea and the running test, Captain Smith opened it up, and the ship steamed south for two hours, averaging 18 knots, and even hitting 21 knots at one point. Returning to Belfast as the sun was setting, the Board of Trade's representatives asked for one last test: both port and starboard anchors were dropped. Satisfied with what he had seen, the board's surveyor, Francis Carruthers, approved the ship.

There was a flurry of activity as assorted Harland and Wolff workers, who had been aboard for the trials but were not heading out with the liner, departed, and a few last-minute supplies were brought onboard. Shortly after 8:00 p.m., the ship raised her anchors and got under way, headed for Southampton, her home port from now on, thirty hours away.

Above: On April 2, 1912, almost a year after launching, *Titanic* heads out for sea trials. After a few hours steaming on Belfast Lough, and speed runs on the Irish Sea, White Star took formal possession of their newest and grandest liner.

CHAPTER THREE

Light, Space, and Luxury

When you see them, you are sure they're champagne bottles right away.

Maybe it's the bottles' lines, those sloping shoulders with that concave bottom. The other giveaway is the mushroom-shaped corks in the bottles' mouths. Almost all the other wine bottles found in *Titanic*'s debris field no longer have their corks in place. The pressure of the sea at that depth pushed them in long ago. But with champagne, rather than forcing the cork in as the bottle sinks, the water works its way through it, expelling any air, but preserving cork and bottle alike.

And, of course, they have to be champagne bottles. That fits with some half-understood ideas we have about lost splendor, all mixed up in our minds with images of men in evening dress puffing big cigars in rooms filled with potted palms. It represents, in short, what we think of when we use the word Edwardian. Edward VII was two years dead by the time *Titanic* took to the sea, but never mind; the ship was begun while he was still on the throne, and the spirit of his reign permeated the ship.

It is a series of clichés, but they aren't completely off-base. *Titanic* was, above all else, luxurious. She wasn't the first no-holds-barred, no-expense-spared luxury ship; probably some of the French and German liners could claim that, and her great Cunard rivals were nicely appointed, too. As well, the Cunard ships could squeeze out a couple of knots more per hour, about 26, in contrast to *Titanic* and *Olympic*'s more modest 21 knots. Over the distance between Queenstown, Ireland (their traditional last stop in the Old World), to Sandy Hook, outside New York City (about 2890 nautical miles),

Relics photographed in *Titanic*'s debris field, including what seems to be a chamber pot. The conventional wine bottles have lost their corks — the pressure 2.5 miles down pushed them in — but the champagne bottles in the center are still intact.

Right: Another champagne bottle, here nestled next to a woman's shoe.

Below: This open window belongs to Stateroom U. Some of *Titanic*'s first-class rooms featured conventional windows, not ports, a luxurious if quite un-nautical touch.

that worked out to a total elapsed time of 116 hours for the Cunarders, compared to 137 for *Titanic* and *Olympic*, a difference of almost a day.

White Star's approach was to take things a little slower than the rough-sailing Cunard ships. By the time *Titanic* was launched, crossing the Atlantic hadn't really been a brutal ordeal, one where the passengers prayed avidly for the voyage to be over, or if they were seasick (a common occurrence), for death, at the very least, to come quickly. But *Olympic* and *Titanic* were two of the first ships to acknowledge that getting there might be, if not half the fun (as later ads for transatlantic voyaging put it), at least not a test of the will and the stomach. In this approach, *Titanic* differed from some of her contemporaries and shared more in common with the luxurious super liners of the 1930s, or even modern cruise ships which, sailing pretty well without destination, can worry exclusively about the care, feeding, and amusement of their passengers.

Titanic's luxury was more than a case of good food and wine, although the liner could boast plenty of that — among the items stocking her larder on her maiden voyage were more than 1,500 bottles of wine and 20,000 of beer and stout, 75,000 pounds of fresh meat, 800 bundles of asparagus, and more than 1,700 quarts of ice cream. More can be said, and will be, about the food on *Titanic*, but for now, if you really want to know what set *Titanic* so far apart from other ships, you should consider another object in the debris field, created when the ship split in two and scattered so many objects across the ocean floor.

Left: More conventional wine bottles on the bottom, minus their corks, and (right) what look like Chianti bottles. All these bottles would have landed on the bottom in wooden cases. Their crates have long since disappeared, leaving these intriguing groupings on the sea floor.

It is twisted and bent now and, looking at it, it seems probable that it is made out of some sort of soft metal, something delicate that had been formed into a circular pattern. In fact, it's a skylight. To be more specific, it is a circular, dome-shaped skylight, one of two such onboard. They surmounted, or perhaps crowned is a grander and more accurate way of putting it, the forward and aft first-class staircases, letting natural light pour into these public spaces.

What *Titanic* offered her passengers that was truly luxurious were qualities that had historically been scarce on ships: space and, secondarily, light.

Below: The delicate remains of one of the two glass domes that graced *Titanic*'s forward and aft first-class staircases.

Below: Similar details can be made out in this photograph of the dome over the ship's forward first-class staircase.

Bottom: The ornately carved clock depicted allegorical figures of Honor and Glory crowning Time. It was located on the forward first-class staircase's topmost landing, just under the dome.

Overleaf: The entrance to the forward first-class staircase today.

A brief digression makes this a little clearer. Consider *Olympic* and *Titanic*'s great rivals *Lusitania* and *Mauretania*. The Cunarders were the smaller ships, a little under 800 feet long and displacing about 31,500 gross tons. The *Olympic* and *Titanic* were nearly 100 feet longer at 882 feet, and displaced 53,000 tons. They were bigger and, more important, emptier. *Lusitania* and *Mauretania* were designed to carry 552 first-class passengers, 460 second-class passengers, and 1,186 in third class, for a total of 2,198 passengers. As designed, however, *Olympic* and *Titanic* carried 2,389 passengers in all classes — not even two hundred more people on ships fifty percent bigger than their nearest rivals (by gross tonnage, a measure of volume not weight). There was plenty of room to stretch out.

That space was an essential element of *Titanic*'s magic would have been obvious even before you stepped aboard. Most passengers, whatever class they were in, took the boat train from London to Southampton on the morning of their sailing, which in the case of *Titanic*'s maiden voyage was April 10, 1912. The liner had arrived in Southampton on April 4, and the preceding week had been spent supplying the ship and otherwise getting her ready for passengers — bringing aboard food and plants and finishing some last-minute painting. The train came close alongside the new White Star docks, so your first view of the ship would have been of it looming over the line's shed, a vast black-and-white wall the height of a six-story building.

Most first-class passengers entered the ship on D deck, which meant climbing a flight of stairs and then walking across the pier via a covered movable gantry that fed them right into the depths of the liner. At that moment, any previous expectations of what to find on a ship, or what you would have found on a ship even a few years before, would have been immediately confounded. First-class passengers stepped aboard into the ship's reception room, a large, well-appointed sitting room that resembled nothing so much as a public room in a plush hotel. This was not surprising. J. Bruce Ismay, White Star's managing director, had toured the best hotels in England, the United States, and Europe looking for inspiration for his liner. In the

Opposite: *Titanic* at dock side in Southampton, April 10, 1912. The elevated gangway seen here was the one that second-class passengers took to enter the ship.

Below: *Titanic*'s interiors were done in a variety of eclectic fashions, from Jacobean and Regency to pseudo-French café. Her first-class lounge, identical to *Olympic*'s shown here, was done in Louis Quinze style.

Right: A rare photograph showing passengers in Titanic's first-class dining room. Measuring 114 feet long by 92 feet wide, it was the largest room afloat.

white-paneled reception room, which featured comfortable looking wicker tub chairs and round tables, there was nothing, apart from a few signs announcing that you were on D deck, to suggest you were on a ship.

As well as functioning as a sort of seaborne lobby, the reception room also served as an antechamber, where passengers would gather before entering the ship's grand first-class dining room. Here, again, the scale of the ship was apparent. This dining space was the largest room afloat, an Edwardian take on Louis XV Versailles style, variously described as inspired by the great English country house Haddon Hall or copied directly from it. The room measured 114 feet long by 92 feet wide. Featuring leaded glass windows and private little Jacobean-style alcoves, it could seat about 550 people at a time.

Titanic boasted a number of other impressive public spaces in first class. Further astern, there was an à la carte restaurant for those passengers who found the dining room a bit stuffy, or who, and this was without precedent on an Atlantic liner, wanted to dine on their own, not at a pre-arranged table. There was a lounge and, farther aft, a first-class smoking room that, with its paneled walls and green leather chairs, looked like a private London men's club, and was in fact a male-only preserve. But by far the most impressive space of all was not a room but the forward first-class staircase, often referred to as the grand staircase.

From the reception room on D deck, the twin set of curved stairs swept up and around, each floor opening into spacious entrance halls lit by gold-plated crystalline light fixtures, and featuring arrange-

ments of attractive, airy-looking wicker furniture. The tiled floors contrasted nicely with the staircase's polished oak paneling and the elaborate gilded balustrades. The very top landing contained a large clock, featuring an allegorical carving showing Honor and Glory crowning Time. And over it all arched the elaborate glass dome, held together by filigree metalwork that let natural light flood down into the ship.

The stairs and dome are long gone now, but even looking at the yawning opening they once occupied lets us appreciate their scale. This was the Main Street of first class, tying together many of the ship's poshest public spaces. All told, it connected five decks, running from the top of the ship down to E deck, home to the Turkish bath and swimming pool, which together with *Titanic*'s squash court was the first ever installed on a ship. The great Norwegian-American economist Thorstein Veblen, when writing about the behavior of America's rich in the gilded age, coined the phrase "conspicuous consumption" to refer to the use of a good or service to prove one's high social standing. *Titanic*'s extravagant grand staircase, with its elegant landings and sitting areas, represented the conspicuous consumption of a ship's most precious commodity: space.

Here, *Titanic* announced, was space in abundance.

Among *Titanic*'s amenities was a gymnasium (left), featuring the most up-to-date exercise equipment, including a mechanical camel, and a Turkish bath (below) done in appropriate "Oriental" style.

Below: The liner *New York* floats within a few feet of *Titanic*. As she passed *New York*, the White Star liner's wake lifted the smaller ship, snapping her lines, and she began drifting into the shipping channel.

Both (left) J. Bruce Ismay, chairman and managing director of the White Star Line, and (right) Thomas Andrews, the head designer for Harland and Wolff, boarded the liner at Southampton on April 10, 1912. The two men were keen to see how the ship would perform on her maiden voyage.

Titanic, maiden voyage or not, was by no means full when, with a blast of her great steam whistles, she dropped her lines and the fleet of attending tugs moved her out into the waters of Southampton's River Test. Partly because some potential passengers had been scared off by the recent coal strike that had cancelled a lot of sailings, and also because April 10 was still a bit early in the season, *Titanic* had not sold out. About 202 first-class, 257 second-class, and 1,109 third-class passengers were aboard. Further passengers would join the ship in Cherbourg and Queenstown in Ireland, but even with the addition of several hundred people, she would still be sailing at only sixty percent of her designed capacity. Among her passengers for the maiden voyage were J. Bruce Ismay and Thomas Andrews, the Harland and Wolff director and head of the company's drafting department who had a major hand in imagining the liner. Both were aboard for this voyage to see how exactly *Titanic* fulfilled White Star's expectations.

The tugs pulled *Titanic* into the Test, where the waters of the dock met the sea channel, and she began moving under her own power. But as the liner steamed down the narrow channel to enter Southampton water, things began to go wrong. Off *Titanic*'s port side were two liners, currently out of service thanks to the coal strike. One of them, *Oceanic (II)*, was tied directly to a dock; the other, *New York*, had been made fast to *Oceanic*'s outboard side. As *Titanic* passed the two liners, the enormous amount of water she displaced seemed to lift the *New York*. The smaller ship's lines tightened, then snapped, and she began drifting into the channel. For one frightening moment, it looked as if the *New York* would collide with *Titanic*'s side, in a replay of *Olympic*'s run-in with the *Hawke*. Captain Smith quickly reversed the engines, and the wake from the port propeller actually pushed the *New York* away. The tugs that had been helping *Titanic* seaward corralled *New York* in fairly short order, easing her past *Titanic* and safely away. The near miss cost *Titanic* an hour's delay, and again raised the question about these big new ships' handling qualities.

While there were small variations in design between *Olympic* and *Titanic* (for example, the painting in *Olympic*'s first-class lounge showed New York harbor, while the painting hung in the same location in the lounge on *Titanic* showed Plymouth, England), the two ships had been planned, essentially, as identical twins. But while she was being built, White Star began to modify *Titanic* in light of what the company was learning from *Olympic* on her first runs. Both ships had been designed with three promenades for the first- and second-class passengers: the open boat deck atop the ship, the appropriately named promenade deck immediately below that, and finally the bridge deck. On *Titanic*, White Star decided to convert the enclosed promenade on the bridge deck into first-class cabins, twenty-eight in all, many in keeping with the ship's grand hotel feel, featuring not portholes but conventional windows. Two of the ship's most luxurious cabins, the parlor suites, were also located here. Each had a sitting room, two bedrooms, two wardrobe rooms for clothes, and a private bathroom, and featured their very own promenades 50 feet in length. Having taken over *Titanic*'s enclosed promenade, White Star then modified the remaining promenade by enclosing it, which made it usable in the colder winter months. Perhaps because so few pictures were taken of *Titanic* during her brief career, pictures of *Olympic* are frequently misidentified as *Titanic*. But *Olympic*'s open promenade deck is easy to spot. A few years ago, a book was published that claimed White Star had switched *Olympic* and *Titanic* as part of an insurance scheme, and *Olympic* had gone to the bottom, not her sister. *Titanic* carried on as *Olympic* for another two decades on the North Atlantic under her sister's name. *Titanic*'s enclosed promenade deck, so clearly visible today on the wreck, puts paid to this rather silly theory.

Even with the loss of the bridge deck promenades, *Titanic* boasted a tremendous amount of open or semi-open space for her passengers, particularly those in first class, to enjoy. The promenade deck was itself over 500 feet long, and the boat deck had a 200-foot-long area reserved for first-class passengers alone.

Below: In this photograph showing *Olympic* in New York, the promenade deck is clearly open. In *Titanic*, this was enclosed so passengers could enjoy it in bad weather.

Left: Six-year-old Robert Douglas Spedden spins a top on the aft promenade deck, reserved for first-class passengers. Overleaf: *Titanic*'s distinctive enclosed promenade deck as it looks today.

Top: One of *Titanic*'s first-class staterooms. Although undeniably luxurious, most of them didn't have their own baths — that was a feature that would not be standard on liners for a few years yet.

Middle: *Titanic*'s first class set a new standard, but second class wasn't bad, either. A little more businesslike, but still pleasant, as this photograph of *Titanic*'s second-class smoking room shows.

Bottom: Titanic's third-class dining room. If first class resembled a great private house and second class had the feeling of a good British railway hotel, third class still said ship.

This was also where the ship's gymnasium was located, an airy room with high arched windows where first-class passengers could work out on rowing machines and stationary bicycles as well as trying out the novel mechanical camel. The boat deck was also home to the ship's lifeboats. There were sixteen standard boats in all, as required by the British Board of Trade for any vessel over 10,000 tons, and *Titanic* carried four collapsible boats in addition to this. The broad, open boat decks were popular with passengers, and perhaps as a result, most shipping lines were reluctant to clutter them up with lifeboats and davits. Second-class passengers had the use of the rear end of the boat deck for an open-air promenade and further areas on the next two decks down. Third class, more than one thousand people in all, made do with a small area at the rear of the ship on the poop deck.

When talking about the classes on *Titanic*, there is always a tendency to view the ship as an enormous floating metaphor for the society that created it — the rich at the top, a small middle class, then a vast third-class peasantry physically and figuratively beneath their betters. Imagining the stokers sweating away in the ship's engine rooms adds a final, hellish touch. It's a nice image, but it's not quite accurate. The highest-placed accommodation in the ship, the boat deck, was for the ship's officers, who needed to be near the bridge. A, B, and C decks were exclusively for first-class cabins, true, but the second-class public rooms were also on B and C decks. D and E decks had first-, second- and third-class cabins, and F and G were second and third class. But, while the classes might share decks, it was not easy to move between their different areas.

Actually, what *Titanic* resembled in some ways was a time machine. Her first class was the future of shipboard accommodation, the floating hotel, the standard against which all liners would from here on be judged. *Titanic*'s second class was the equal of first class on pretty much any other ship afloat. Very comfortable, but still undeniably nautical — in her spacious second-class dining room, the tables and chairs were fixed in place to stop them from sliding about in heavy weather. This long-standing feature of shipboard life had been done away with in her first-class dining room. Second-class cabins were pleasant, too, but there was no attempt to make you feel you had wandered into a French chateau or a Regency townhouse.

When you entered *Titanic*'s third class, you really knew you were aboard a ship. The cabins had bunks, the white enameled walls of the third-class dining room were decorated with White Star posters, and what natural light there was came not from skylights or windows but genuine portholes. In the third-class general room there were wooden benches and captain's chairs, but no wicker furniture or potted palms. Austere, yes, but it compared favorably with even the first-class accommodation of just a few decades before. Obviously, White Star wanted the wealthy passengers, the ones who could typically afford to spend eighty-seven pounds for a cabin (or up to 660 pounds for one of the parlor suites), and the line made sure the wealthy got their money's worth. But third class was no afterthought. In the days when the United States was taking a million or more new immigrants every year, with the majority arriving from Europe via ship, those huddled masses were a steady moneymaker. How much of a moneymaker became clear in the 1920s when the United States government severely limited immigration and the lines had to scramble to find new revenue.

When we scan the debris field, we see, perhaps, first a pot, then a pitcher not far away or, here, a tea cup and, over there, a serving dish. So much of this sad detritus seems to be connected to food.

Below: A second-class stateroom on *Olympic*. Note the odd shape of the wash basin. They were designed to flip up into the bureau when not in use. This modification meant the water could drain out after the sink was raised.

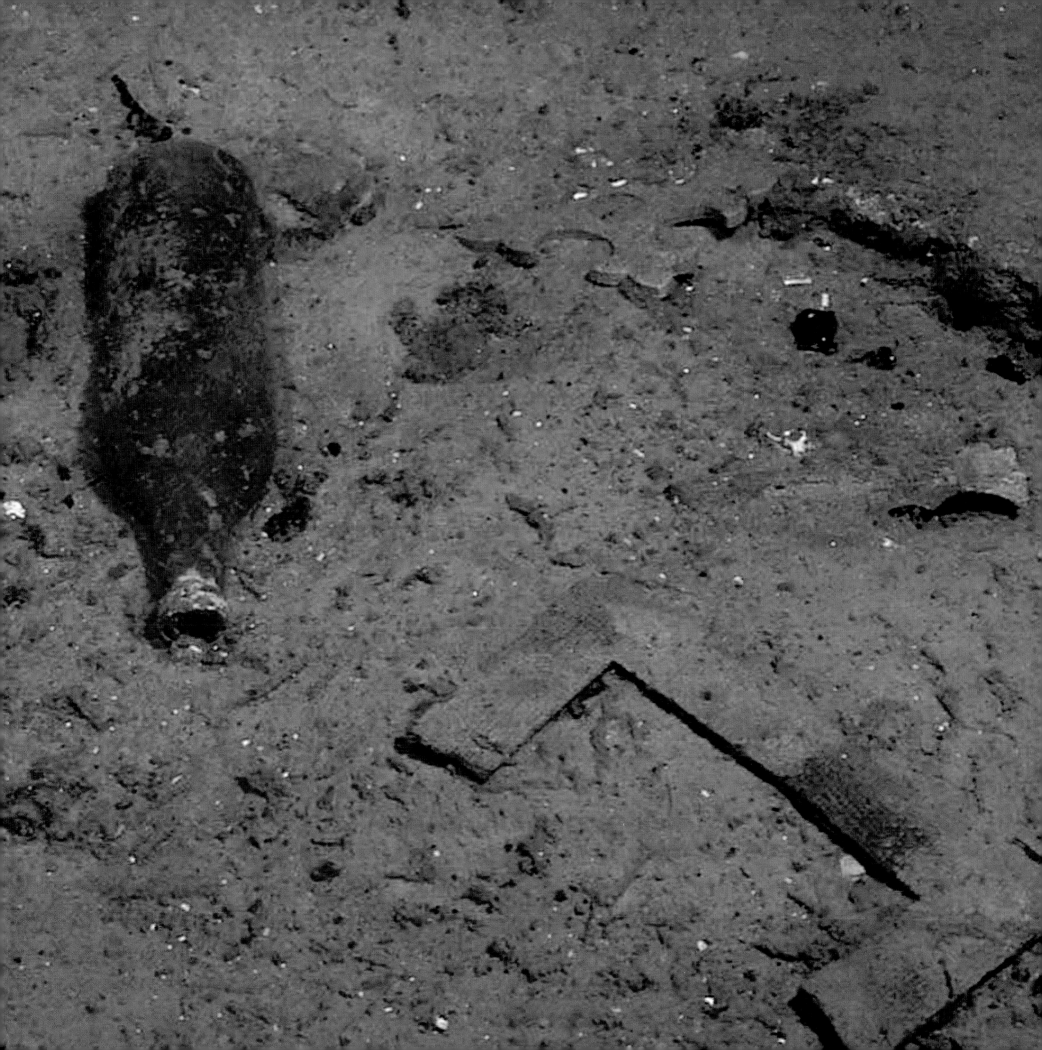

Previous page: A marine animal clings to one of *Titanic*'s plates in the debris field. Because they are china or metal, a lot of objects related to food and eating, such as (below) this stack of metal trays, (bottom) this copper cooking pot and (opposite) this attractive pitcher, have survived more than ninety years on the bottom.

Partly what we're seeing is the shipwreck's equivalent of survival of the fittest: metal pots and serving plates, glass bottles, china dishes and bowls have survived far better than organic materials like cloth and wood. But it also represents a truth about *Titanic*.

As it is today on a cruise liner, food was an incredibly important part of an Atlantic crossing. In addition to having a dining room for each class, *Titanic* also boasted an à la carte restaurant, a verandah café and the Café Parisien, a shipboard version of a sidewalk café, complete with French waiters. The meals were elaborate, the portions were large and there was plenty of choice. The first-class menu for April 14, 1912, boasted seven courses, including a choice for the entrée of lamb, roast duckling, or sirloin of beef, followed by punch romaine and either roast squab, cold asparagus vinaigrette, or pâté de foie gras, and then dessert. Food in second class (which shared the first-class kitchen) was nearly as sumptuous, and even third-class food, if not fancy, was certainly plentiful. For the ship's steerage-class passengers, a typical day's eating might kick off with oatmeal, or perhaps fried tripe and onions, followed by a dinner (lunch) of roast beef and boiled potatoes, with rabbit pie for tea (dinner). To feed her passengers, *Titanic* carried sixty chefs and chefs' assistants, including bakers and pastry chefs and even a kosher chef to prepare meals for the ship's Jewish passengers. The ship also boasted thirty-six full-time glassmen, plate washers and scullerymen to wash up after meals. In fact, chefs, dishwashers and scullery men outnumbered the more conventional seamen onboard ship, those crew members whose duties were to handle lines, help the officers navigate, and man the boats.

Opposite: *Titanic* pulls away from Queenstown (now Cobh). Snapped by Francis M. Browne, a young candidate for the Jesuit order who left the ship in Ireland, this is the last known picture of the liner.

Eating was one of the dominant pastimes on *Titanic* because there really wasn't much else to do. *Titanic* did have some of the trappings that we associate with later liners and modern cruise ships — the gymnasium on the boat deck, the squash court, and the swimming pool — but their dimensions were modest, limiting their use, and they were restricted to one class. The era of the ocean liner as an endless series of distractions, with cinemas, beauty parlors, stores, dances, even spirited games of shuffleboard, was still a decade away. Instead, *Titanic* assumed a far more passive sort of leisure. Passengers read, played cards, or walked the areas of the deck reserved for them, perhaps renting a deck chair if they were in first or second class. There, wrapped in a warm steamer blanket, they might quietly snooze in the weak April sunlight. Above all, they ate.

This agreeable routine would have established itself quickly aboard *Titanic*. After leaving Southampton, *Titanic* headed for Cherbourg in France, where she picked up an additional 274 passengers, ferried out to the ship by two White Star-owned tenders, the *Nomadic* and the *Traffic*. Given that it was her maiden voyage and that Captain Smith did have a reputation as the millionaire's captain, it is not surprising that a number of rich people had chosen to sail on her. Three noteworthy American plutocrats who joined the ship at Cherbourg were Benjamin Guggenheim, Margaret Tobin Brown (better known as Mollie), the wife of a Denver mining millionaire, and John Jacob Astor. One of the world's richest men, he was traveling with his young bride Madeleine. Astor had created a scandal a few years before by divorcing his wife, and created another one a few years later by marrying Madeleine. He had left the United States to let things cool down and, after some months abroad, was returning with his now-pregnant bride. Also boarding the ship at Cherbourg were Sir Cosmo Duff Gordon and his wife, better known as "Lucile," who was one of the leading fashion designers of the day. They joined a number of other wealthy Americans who had boarded the ship at Southampton, including Isidor Straus, one of the founders of Macy's department store, and his wife Ida, and George Widener, heir to Philadelphia's largest fortune.

Titanic's pause at Cherbourg was brief — just about ninety minutes — and by 8:10 p.m. she was underway. From there, the ship headed for Queenstown, reaching the Irish port at 11:30 a.m. on April 11 and anchoring two miles off shore. Tenders carried 1,385 sacks of mail and 120 passengers to the ship, bringing back seven passengers who had planned to sail only as far as Ireland. The great liner now had 2,207 passengers and crew onboard. A little more than two hours after she had arrived, *Titanic* raised her anchor. At 1:55, *Titanic* gave three long blasts with her steam whistles and began heading westward, along the Irish coast.

Her next stop was America.

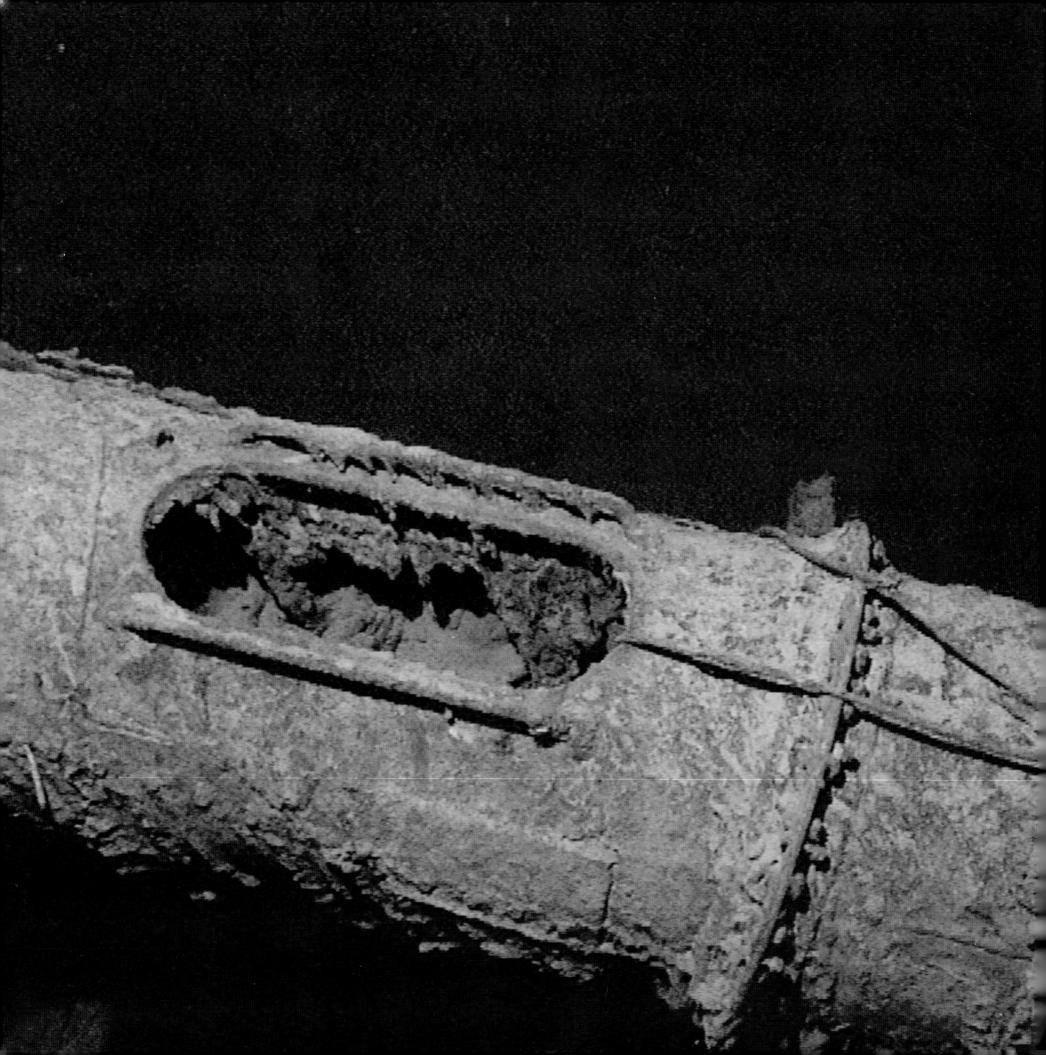

CHAPTER FOUR

THE SINKING

TITANIC'S FOREMAST IS one of the places where you can see just how badly the wreck has been damaged since we discovered the ship in 1985. Look at a picture of this area from twenty years ago, and the crow's nest, albeit battered and bent, was still in place, as was the crow's nest telephone and the mast-head light. Since then, the crow's nest has been torn away, and salvagers have taken both the masthead light and the telephone. What is now more visible, however, is the small opening in the mast that the lookouts used to enter the crow's nest. *Titanic*'s 205-foot-tall foremast was hollow, and to reach the crow's nest, which was 90 feet above the water, you climbed up a ladder inside it.

Titanic could boast of six lookouts who worked in two-man teams, scanning the sea from the crow's nest for two hours at a stretch and then taking four hours off. On the night of April 14, 1912, the watch in the crow's nest had changed at 10:00 p.m., and Frederick Fleet and Reginald Lee were not long into their shift when the ship hit the iceberg. It may have been defensiveness on his part (and as the man who spotted the iceberg, but not quite soon enough, Lookout Frederick Fleet certainly had plenty to be defensive about), but at the British inquiry into the sinking, Fleet maintained that had he had a set of binoculars, he would certainly have spotted the iceberg in time. Though there had been a set of binoculars in the crow's nest when the ship left Belfast, on arrival at Southampton, one of the lookouts gave them to Second Officer Davy Blair (presumably for safekeeping), who was replaced by Herbert Lightoller, and never sailed. The binoculars never made it to the lookouts, and rest in Blair's former cabin undersea to this day.

Left: The opening in *Titanic*'s hollow foremast that the lookouts used to enter the now-missing crow's nest.
Overleaf: The base *of Titanic*'s foremast rests on the forecastle deck, still generally where it stood when upright.

Left: *Titanic*'s crow's nest as it looked in 1912, with its warning bell mounted above the entrance that is shown on page 76.

Right: *Titanic*'s boat deck shown in a White Star brochure. The weather for her maiden voyage was calm and sunny, and passengers would have taken advantage of the ship's spacious boat deck, as they are doing here.

Right: The crow's nest as it looked when I discovered the ship in 1985.

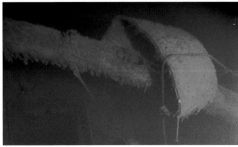

Right: Frederick Fleet, on duty as a lookout the night *Titanic* sank, later claimed that with binoculars he would have seen the iceberg in time. He had mentioned their disappearance to Second Officer Herbert Lightoller, who passed it on to First Officer William Murdoch, but that was the end of it.

One of the lookouts complained about the missing glasses to Second Officer Herbert Lightoller, who in turn had spoken to First Officer William Murdoch about them, but there the matter seems to have ended, and the lookouts made do without them.

Would it have made a difference if *Titanic*'s lookouts had had their binoculars that night? Perhaps. But, in general, lookouts scanned the horizon with the naked eye and, when they saw something, used their binoculars for a closer look. Still, it's a tantalizing what-if. But so many of the events surrounding the sinking fall into the category of tantalizing what-ifs. Thomas Hardy entitled his poem on the *Titanic*'s loss "The Convergence of the Twain." A great poem, but sending *Titanic* to the bottom required more than liner and iceberg to converge. A series of conditions had to be met, were met, that ensured at the critical moment that the tragedy was all but inevitable.

After leaving Ireland behind, *Titanic*'s speed had opened up. The Atlantic, at least on this particular week in April, was calm and the weather was clear, and soon the ship was piling up the miles — 484 from noon on April 11 to noon on April 12, and 519 the next day. One first-class passenger, Elizabeth Lines, recalls sitting in the D-Deck reception area and hearing Ismay speaking to Captain Smith in a "dictatorial fashion," telling him that they would not only beat *Olympic*'s crossing speed, they would arrive in New York a day early. *Titanic* was making 22.5 knots, perhaps even more. Another passenger recalls Ismay telling them that on April 14, two more boilers were lit, which would have helped the ship squeeze out even more speed.

April has historically been the worst month of the year for icebergs. Thanks to warmer spring temperatures, they begin breaking

off Greenland's glaciers, and then slowly drifting south on the ocean current. On April 12, *Titanic* began receiving reports from other ships via her wireless of lone icebergs and even large fields of ice — a mixture of icebergs, growlers (low-lying icebergs), and smaller chunks of floating ice. Ships crossing westward across the Atlantic at this time of year usually headed farther south from the normal shipping lanes to avoid the ice, before reaching a point in the ocean referred to as "the corner," where they would turn and proceed due west. On receiving this first ice message, Smith decided to head farther south, and actually took a more southerly route than most ships commonly did. This should have helped them avoid most ice, but 1912 seems to have been a particularly bad year, and ships were encountering icebergs and drifting ice much farther south than was normally the case.

Smith wouldn't have known this, of course, but he might have worked it out from the sheer number of ice warnings *Titanic* received. The recently introduced wireless was a helpful tool for any ship's captain, particularly concerning a navigational challenge like ice, where you want up-to-date, first-hand information. But perhaps because wireless was so new, people hadn't yet worked out procedures for making sure that the information received reached those who needed it. In fact, *Titanic*'s wireless operators were not even employees of the White Star Line, but worked for the Marconi Company. They were supposed to make sure that the captain and officers were aware of any message that might be important for the safety of the ship, but most of their time was taken up sending personal messages from the passengers. And at three dollars for the first ten words, and thirty-five cents for each additional one, this was definitely worth their while. Throughout the day on Sunday, April 14, *Titanic* received four more warnings about the ice — one at 9:00 a.m. from the eastbound liner *Caronia*, which Captain Smith posted on the bridge. A Dutch liner made a similar report around 11:40, then, at 1:42, the White Star liner *Baltic* reported a large field of ice about 250 miles ahead of *Titanic,* which was repeated by a German liner a

The only known photograph of *Titanic*'s wireless room, taken by Francis M. Browne, shows junior operator Harold Bride working the key.

Opposite: The square opening here was the skylight for *Titanic*'s Marconi Room. The ship's two operators, Jack Phillips and Harold Bride (above, left and right), received multiple ice warnings on April 14.

Right: An ice warning received
by *Titanic* from the German liner
Amerika. The ship's wireless
operators dutifully relayed it to
other nearby ships, but it was a
critical warning never brought
on the bridge.

few minutes later. Captain Smith picked up *Baltic's* warning on his way down to lunch, with the intention of posting it on the bridge later. On his way, however, he ran into J. Bruce Ismay and gave it to him, thinking he might be interested. Mrs. Ryerson, a first-class passenger, later remembered Ismay showing it to her with the comment, "We are in among the icebergs." Smith retrieved this message ultimately and took it to the bridge. He never got the second warning, apparently because it wasn't specifically addressed to the captain. Three additional warnings came that evening: one from the ship *Californian* that Bride, one of the wireless operators, delivered to the bridge. No one posted it or showed it to the captain. Another came through at 9:30, but operator Jack Phillips put it aside — he had an enormous backlog of personal telegrams to send and, as far as he knew, the bridge had already been given three previous ice warnings. Finally, at 10:55, *Californian* again contacted *Titanic,* reporting that the ship was stopped and completely surrounded by ice. Phillips cut off *Californian's* wireless operator, telling him to shut up because he was working Cape Race, the wireless station in Newfoundland. No single warning would have tipped off *Titanic* but, taken together, their frequency and the extent of ice they mentioned might have given Smith or his officers pause.

To missing binoculars, extensive amounts of ice, and a haphazard treatment of repeated warnings, must be added the weather. As said, it had been clear and calm for most of the voyage. The night of April 14 was, at least one surviving sailor would later recall, the calmest he had ever seen on the North Atlantic. That it was clear made it easier to see any problem ahead, but the lack of any movement of the sea meant that the lookouts were working without two of the best warnings of icebergs they could have. They couldn't hear waves breaking against its base, nor would they be able to spot telltale bioluminescence, the glow of countless small sea creatures disturbed by waves slapping against an iceberg's sides. As well, it was a moonless night, which meant no light reflecting off any potential hazard.

Left: An illustration from the *Illustrated London News* showing the ice field *Titanic* was heading for, which stretched nearly 80 miles directly in front of her.

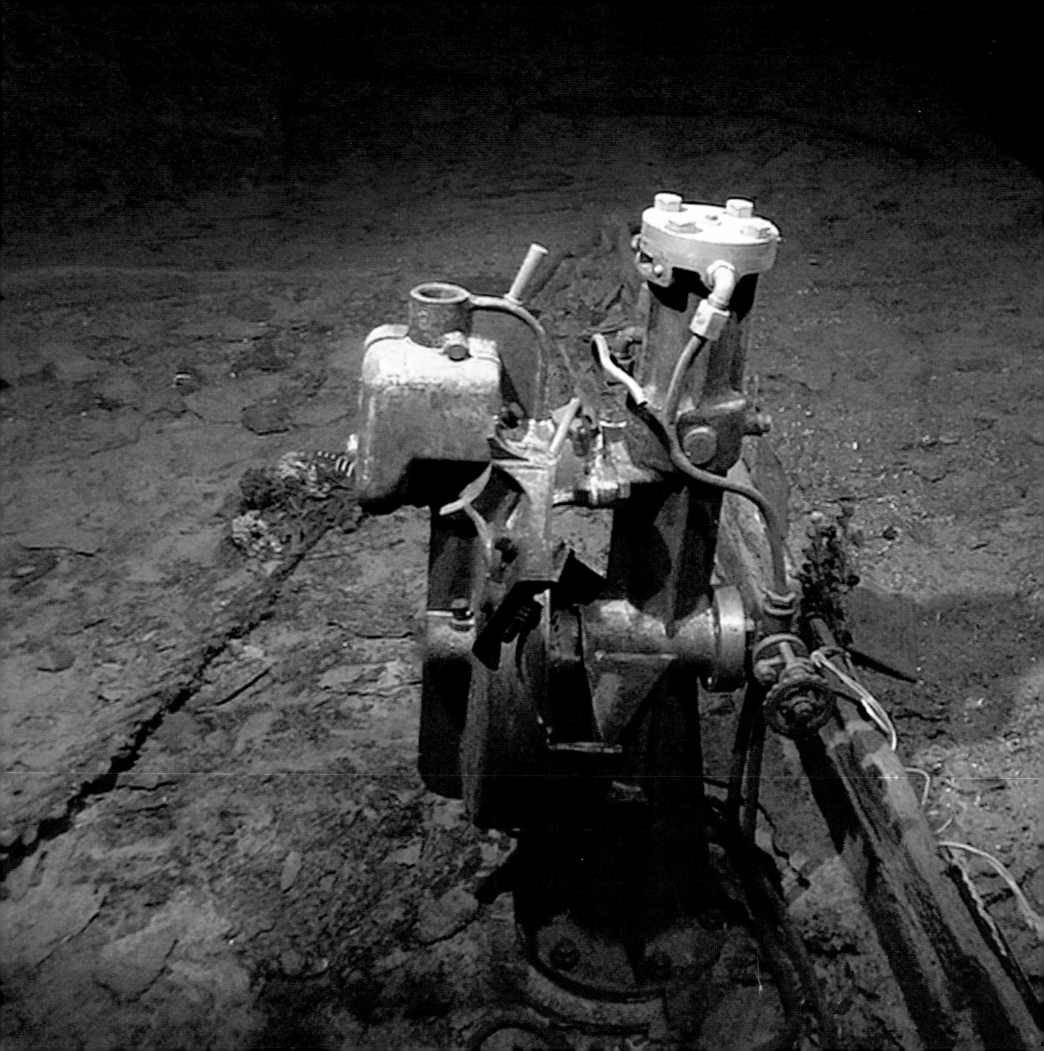

Because it was made of bronze, *Titanic*'s telemotor is still intact, largely unaffected by more than ninety years on the bottom. Originally, it held the ship's wheel and sat in the middle of the wheelhouse, which was itself a sort of room within the covered area of the bridge. The telemotor was a hydraulic device connected to the ship's steering mechanism in the stern. Of course, the ship's wheel it once held, being wood, was long ago eaten away. Indeed, most of the bridge is gone now, torn off as the ship began its final plunge. We can, however, still see a raised lip on the deck here, likely teak, which wood borers don't much like. It shows us where the sides of the wheelhouse were, and with that, the telemotor and a little imagination, we can reconstruct what happened next.

On the bridge after 10:00 that night, Quartermaster Robert Hichens was at the wheel. He would have been standing behind where the telemotor can be seen here. He wouldn't actually have been spending much time looking out. Rather his attention would have been largely focused on the compass ahead of him. Quartermaster Alfred Olliver would have been standing by to take the wheel if Hichens needed it, or to help in any other way. Three officers were also on watch: First Officer William Murdoch, Fourth Officer Joseph Boxhall and Sixth Officer James Moody. They, too, would have been watching ahead quite carefully.

Left: Its bronze still bright, *Titanic*'s telemotor stands alone on the bridge today, long after the wheelhouse and the wheel itself have vanished.
Above: *Titanic*'s telemotor seen with the ship's wheel in place.

Was this the iceberg that sank *Titanic*? Photographed April 15, 1912, not far from where she went down, eyewitnesses reported a smudge of red paint — like that used on the great liner's bottom — along its base.

Frederick Fleet spotted an iceberg directly ahead at 11:39 p.m. Fleet rang the bell as a warning, reached across his fellow lookout and grabbed the phone that connected to the bridge. Moody picked up the telephone and heard Fleet report, "Iceberg right ahead." He rather automatically thanked him, and then yelled a warning to First Officer Murdoch, who had just seen the iceberg himself. Murdoch raced to the ship's telegraph and rang down to the engine room: "Stop." This was followed almost immediately by "Full speed astern." He ordered Quartermaster Hichens, "Hard a starboard," that is, turn the wheel to starboard, which actually would swing the ship to port. The telemotor transferred this movement to the steering mechanism, and the ship slowly began to turn. Murdoch also threw the switch that shut the doors between the ship's watertight compartments.

A few more feet, and probably no one would ever have known a thing about it. Somebody would have had to say something to Captain Smith, and perhaps a brief colorless entry made in the log, "Iceberg sighted, passed at 11:40," but it would likely have gone no further. No need to wake Mr. Ismay, really, is there? Conversely, if they had slammed straight into the iceberg, the ship would likely have survived. But again, the amazing possibilities continued to pile up. When Murdoch reversed the engines, the ship began to slow. Not a great deal, just enough to slow down her turn (the more speed a ship has, the faster she turns). A bit faster and she might have made her turn. For landlubbers, it is hard sometimes to understand how fragile ice could damage a steel ship. But in such a contest, *Titanic* could only lose. Eyewitnesses claimed that the iceberg that *Titanic* scraped along was higher than the boat deck, which was 60 feet above the water. Given that ninety percent of an iceberg is typically below water, this particular iceberg probably extended down several hundred feet into the ocean. The sheer bulk of this iceberg made it like hitting a rock at very high speed. As *Titanic* scraped along the side of the iceberg, the steel plates of her hull began to buckle, popping out rivets. The scrape opened up six of her watertight compartments.

From sighting to impact took only thirty-seven seconds.

Titanic originally carried sixteen pairs of Welin davits, eight pairs on each side of the ship, for her sixteen lifeboats. Almost all are gone now, torn off the ship when she sank or rusted away over the years. There are perhaps three still in position on the ship today. Two are found on the port side. There is one which originally lowered the ship's No. 8 boat. This particular davit is swung out over the side of the ship and still seems to have the block through which the lines used to lower the boat would have run. Forward stands one of the davits for the No. 2 boat. It has lost its block, but you can see at its base some of the mechanism for moving the davit.

The Welin davit was relatively new when *Titanic* was being built, and when we look at it, we are looking at yet one more of those tantalizing, depressing missed opportunities in the *Titanic* story.

Titanic carried sixteen lifeboats under her davits. Fourteen large ones, capable of holding sixty-five people, and two smaller boats kept forward in the No. 1 and No. 2 boat positions, just aft of the bridge. These smaller boats were usually kept swung outboard on the ship and were for ready use in the case of an emergency, specifically a man overboard. These two more modest boats carried a maximum of forty people each. *Titanic* was also equipped with four collapsible boats, craft with wooden bottoms but canvas sides that would be raised before launching. Two were stored on deck beside the Nos. 1 and 2 boats; two more were kept on the cabin housing the officer's quarters on the boat deck, on either side of the first funnel. These four craft were above and beyond the requirements of the Board of Trade.

But Andrew Carlisle, the retired chairman of Harland and Wolff who had a hand in the work on *Titanic*, had made allowances for the ship to carry many more boats. The original regulations for lifeboats ruled that only those that were, as they said, under davits, met the Board of Trade's requirements. This was understandable. Wooden lifeboats were very heavy. To launch one that was not carried on davits, but was stored inboard, would have required manhandling the boat into place. Traditionally, if you wanted more lifeboats,

Left: An advertisement for the Welin davits, boasting of their use on the liners *Olympic* and *Titanic*.
Below: Welin davits in place on another ship of the time.

Left: *Titanic* photographed from water level at Queenstown. Of *Titanic*'s sixteen regulation lifeboats, two were smaller craft carried in the forwardmost davits and usually swung out for immediate use. One of these, Boat No. 1, is visible here, just behind the bridge.

that meant more sets of davits. The Welin davit, however, resembled a crane more than a traditional curved boat davit. It could swing out a boat, lower it, and then its arms could be cranked far inboard to pick up another. A single pair of Welin davits could launch several boats. *Titanic*'s sixteen boats met the regulations of the day but, evidently, Carlisle himself became worried that these regulations did not reflect the number of passengers the new, larger liners could carry. So at one stage in the design process, Carlisle suggested that *Titanic* carry up to sixty-four boats, and worked up a design showing it with forty-eight, sixteen under davits and thirty-two spares. The boat deck would have been slightly more cluttered, true, but there would still have been a fair amount of the deck left open for the enjoyment of the passengers. More important, *Titanic*'s lifeboat capacity would have increased, from 1,178 to 1,700. In an interview after the sinking, Carlisle said that he had presented the idea for more boats to two of the directors of the White Star Line, only to have it rejected.

One of those directors, Carlisle remembered, was J. Bruce Ismay.

Each boat on *Titanic* had its own story. And while Walter Lord dubbed the disaster "A Night to Remember," what people did remember varied according to where they were on the ship at differing times. The memories are fragmentary and contradictory. It's hard to know where to begin. Well, we have the davits for the two boats. Perhaps we should start there.

Boats Nos. 2 and 8 were located on the port side (port side boats were even numbered, starboard boats, odd). On either side of the ship, *Titanic*'s lifeboats were arranged in groups of four. Both of these boats were in the forward group. Boat No. 2 was the first in line and Boat No. 8 was the last. As mentioned, Boat No. 2 was up near the bridge, just under the first funnel, beside the officers' staterooms. The No. 8 boat stood just outside the entrance to the first-class staircase. Both were in a section of the boat deck normally reserved for first-class passengers.

Left: One of the surviving davits on the port side. This one, located just behind the bridge, was for the No. 2 boat, and in case of emergency would also be used to launch two of the four collapsible boats that *Titanic* carried. **Overleaf:** The surviving davit from Boat No. 8, located near the entrance to the first-class staircase on the port side.

Second Officer Charles Herbert Lightoller was in charge of loading the port side boats, including No. 8 and No. 2. A stickler for the unwritten law of the sea, Lightoller insisted that only women and children enter the boats under his command.

That *Titanic* was doomed after hitting the iceberg was almost immediately evident. Moments after the collision (which passengers described variously depending on where they were in the ship, as everything from "a tremendous noise" to "a faint grinding jar"), Captain Smith had returned to the bridge from his cabin. Hearing from Murdoch what had happened, he sent off Fourth Officer Boxhall and the ship's carpenter to make an inspection. After receiving reports that the ship was filling rapidly, Smith and Thomas Andrews made a tour of the damaged areas themselves. Andrews knew the ship as well as anyone, and he knew she could float with the first four compartments open to the sea, but not six. One by one, the watertight compartments would fill, and soon the water would begin lapping over the tops of the watertight bulkheads, filling the next compartment and the next, no matter how hard the pumps worked. At 12:05 a.m., after talking with Andrews, Smith ordered the lifeboats uncovered, the first step in getting them ready for launching.

When reading accounts of the sinking, what sticks in the mind is the disorganization. *Titanic* was supposed to have a lifeboat drill that Sunday morning, with all available crew. This was standard on White Star ships. For whatever reason, this Sunday it didn't happen. Some writers have speculated that Captain Smith cancelled it, not wanting the passengers to be aware of the fact that they easily outnumbered the available spots in the lifeboats. Or perhaps it seemed a little pointless in a ship that was, in its own way, an enormous lifeboat. Whatever the case, people were unfamiliar with the lifeboats. Crew members had been assigned specific boats, although the list of these had not been posted until after they left

Queenstown, which means many may not have been aware of which was their charge. There were no assigned boats for passengers, and very little thought was given about how to load them. And even though the ship was clearly doomed, no general alarm was ever given. That was Captain Smith's call, but he never made it. Perhaps, again, he didn't want a riot on his hands. Or maybe he never thought of it. After the collision, Smith seemed to become oddly passive. He told the wireless operators to start sending distress calls but, beyond that, seems to have left the task of saving as many people as possible up to his officers.

The experiences of Boat No. 8 were fairly typical. Crew men started loading passengers into the boat around 12:50. The loading of the portside boats was under the supervision of Second Officer Lightoller, who was very careful about who should be let in. For Lightoller, adhering to the strict law of the sea, it was to be women and children only. Chief Officer Murdoch, supervising the loading of the boats on the starboard side, was a little more forgiving. His policy was women and children first; if there was any room left over, men could enter the boats.

Lightoller wasn't the only man who believed in women and children first. Among those waiting to be helped into Boat No. 8 was Ida Straus, wife of the millionaire Isidor. The two of them had seen her maid into the boat, and Mrs. Straus was about to follow. But with one foot on the gunwale, she suddenly changed her mind. She turned to Isidor, saying, "We have been living together for many years now, and where you go, I go." With that, she stepped back on the deck of the *Titanic*. Despite appeals from other passengers,

Mr. Straus could not be convinced to enter the boat. "I will not go before the other men," he said. With that, the two walked away.

Boat No. 8 was launched at 1:10 a.m., about the same time as Boat No. 1 on the starboard side, making them the fifth and sixth boats to leave the stricken liner. Designed for sixty-five people, it carried twenty-eight. Four of them were men, crew members, in fact, whose job was to steer the boat and row it. Lightoller had originally wanted to send only two off, but because there had already been some trouble launching Boat No. 6 with only two crewmen to work it, Captain Smith had sent along an additional two.

Why so few people? A number of reasons seemed to be at work. Many people were reluctant, especially at this stage so early in the night, to get into a boat. It was cold, the boats weren't all that big, and launching them required being lowered 60 feet on creaking pulleys and squeaking ropes down the side of the ship. Many weren't convinced that the ship was in danger. In part, they had bought into the myth of the unsinkable *Titanic*. Others had been assured by crew members that there was nothing to worry about. And then Lightoller may have been nervous about just exactly how much the ship's davits could support. They worried that lifting a heavy wooden boat with sixty-five people onboard might be too much for them, and the davits would buckle. In fact, they were designed for just such an eventuality, and those on *Olympic* had been tested a year earlier in May 1911, when a boat filled with weight equivalent to sixty-five passengers had been safely raised and lowered six times. No one on *Titanic* seems to have known about this, including Captain Smith and Thomas Andrews. Instead, Lightoller launched the first few boats with fewer people onboard, though he sent a group of seamen down several decks to open a set of doors far down on the side of the ship, where the boats could pull up and take on more passengers. For whatever reason, however, this never occurred.

Perhaps if those doors had been opened, it might have altered one of the starkest facts about Boat No. 8. Although not all of the women in the boat were rich — they included the Strauses' maid and Sarah

Below: Boat No. 8 on deck just forward of the entrance to the first-class staircase. For much of the night, the ship's band would be gathered near here, playing selections to keep people's spirits up.

Left: Survivors from Boat No. 1. Launched at the same time as No. 8, 1:10 a.m., it had a capacity of forty people, but carried only twelve, including Sir and Lady Duff Gordon and seven male crew members.

Below: Seven of the eight members of the Goodwin family from third class.
Bottom: Third-class passengers had a much harder time getting to the boats than those with cabins higher in the ship.

Daniels, who worked for Montreal's Allison family (all but one of whom perished) — they all had cabins in first class. And in that, Boat No. 8 represented, albeit in extreme form, one of the truths of that night: first- and second-class passengers, who were closer to the boat deck to begin with, had a much higher survival rate, proportionately, than third class, who were accommodated farther away, on the lower decks.

Numerous reasons, apart from proximity, have been offered for this sad state of affairs. Perhaps it was snobbery, conscious or unconscious. Something like that had occurred in the *Republic* sinking. *Republic*'s passengers had first transferred to *Florida*, the ship that had rammed her and was herself damaged. When a larger ship arrived and began taking off both *Republic*'s survivors and *Florida*'s passengers, White Star's first-class male passengers had been allowed off the ship ahead of all other passengers — including women and children — from *Florida*. One *Titanic* survivor, Lawrence Beesley, heard an officer direct a woman from second class away from the boats that lined the first-class promenade, telling her to head aft, to the second-class areas. "Your boats, Madam," he explained, "are on your deck." If the first-class boats were in the first-class areas and the second-class boats in the second-class areas, this, of course, begs the question of where, exactly, the third-class boats were.

Then there was the fact that many of the third-class passengers didn't speak English. Once the ship was sinking, they couldn't find their way along *Titanic*'s snaking corridors and up narrow stairways to the boat deck. Oddly, proponents of this theory never explain why the onus in a disaster should fall on the passengers, not the crew. But this doesn't explain the large number of English-speaking third-class passengers who lost their lives that night. They could read the signs, but that didn't help the eight members of the Goodwin family or the eleven members of the Sage family make it into a boat.

More likely, in the end, it is of a piece with everything else that night — the weather, the lack of binoculars, the ignored warnings. Some crew members were telling people there was nothing to worry about, while others were helping passengers into their life jackets and making sure they got on deck. In certain parts of the ship, the gates separating the third-class spaces from other classes were left locked. At other points, third-class passengers were ordered back or held below while half-empty boats left the ship. There was no plan, no rhyme, no reason.

Davits come in pairs, but we have looked at only one of the two on the port side. Let's see what that forward davit can tell us.

Around 1:15, not long after Boat No. 8 set off (with, for most of the night, the Countess of Rothes at the tiller because the seaman who had been given the job proved hopeless), the water reached *Titanic*'s name on the bow. The deck was developing a far more pronounced dip, and even in the absence of a formal general alarm, the earlier indifference was giving way to real consternation. Lightoller recounted that he himself did not realize that the ship was indeed in trouble until he looked down a long stairway, running down four decks from the boat deck, and he could see water slopping at its bottom.

Most of the boats launched after Boat No. 8 tended to be fuller, carrying their full complement, and sometimes even more.

By about 1:40, only one standard boat, No. 4, one smaller emergency boat, No. 2, and the four collapsibles were left on *Titanic*. That equaled about 293 spaces for the more than fifteen hundred people. Although Lightoller was generally in charge of the portside boats, at virtually the same time as No. 2 was being loaded, he was busy one boat aft with Boat No. 4, the one that would carry the young, soon-to-be-widowed Madeleine Astor to safety. Instead, it fell to Boxhall, who had also busied himself that night firing off socket rockets to attract what appeared to be a nearby ship. (Not long after *Titanic* began sinking, crew members had spotted what looked like the masthead lights of a ship just a few miles away. Captain Smith even suggested to the men in charge of Boat No. 8 that they row to the mystery ship, drop off their charges and return. Boxhall tried signaling the ship with a Morse

Left: The Countess of Rothes. Loaded safely into Boat No. 8, once away from the ship she became exasperated with the incompetence of the sailor in charge and wound up handling the tiller for the rest of the night.

Below: Boat No. 4 being loaded from the promenade deck. (Although the details are a trifle off — the deck featured large square ports.) Among its passengers was the pregnant Madeleine Astor, young wife of John Jacob.

lamp, and then firing rockets. Whatever ship was there — some suggested the freighter *Californian* that had been in contact earlier that evening, but this now seems unlikely — it never responded. Its identity remains a mystery to this day.)

Perhaps it was the urgency of trying to get all of the boats away, but No. 2 was not full. Unlike Boat No. 8, however, Boat No. 2 did go off with at least a smattering of third-class passengers, among them Winnie Coutts and her two sons. It had been a near thing for them. Somehow she had threaded her way through the ship from third class with her two sons in tow. Young Willie Coutts, a tall lad, had a straw hat that he was wearing that night. Its effect was to make him look older, desirable perhaps at other times, but nearly fatal on *Titanic*. His mother had to plead for him to be let into the boat.

Boat No. 2 went off at 1:45, but our surviving davit still had work to do. Once Boat No. 4 had been safely released, Lightoller and the group of men who had been helping him all night came forward and began to ready Collapsible D to launch, using No. 2's davits.

Looking at this spot, we can imagine Lightoller and his men struggling to erect the sides of the collapsible and connect it to the falls. Every other boat had now left, including Collapsible C, launched from the starboard No. 1 boat davits. Among its passengers was J. Bruce Ismay, who had, at the last moment, saved himself. Two more collapsibles would float off when the ship sank.

Lightoller had seamen link arms around Collapsible D to hold back the crowds, allowing only women and children to pass through. One man, a Mr. Hoffman, handed his two young sons through. His real name was Michel Navratil. He had kidnapped his two sons, Michel and Edmond, in a ploy to save his failing marriage. As he handed the boys over, he gave them a message for their mother: "Tell her that I loved her and still do. Tell her that I expected her to follow us, so that we might all live happily together..." At approximately 2:05 a.m., Collapsible D began descending. As it passed the promenade deck, two men leapt into the boat from the windows.

Opposite: Boat No. 2's forward davit was also used to launch Collapsible D.

Left: Young Willie Coutts very nearly didn't make it into that boat. His straw boater, which he wears here, made him look older, and his mother had to beg to get him aboard.

Above: They were known as the *Titanic* orphans. Michel (left) and Edmond Navratil (right) had been spirited away by their father after separating from his wife in France.

The boys survived; their father died. After stories appeared worldwide wondering who they were, they were reunited with their mother.

Overleaf: *Titanic*'s port side promenade deck, near where Boat No. 4 loaded.

Most of the stern today is a tangle of smashed and unrecognizable metal. Decks have been torn and twisted, even folded over on themselves. But go to the extreme end of the stern, and it's a different story. You can make out bollards, railings, and recognizably nautical details. And it was here the final act of *Titanic*'s tragedy played out.

Man has long battled the sea. Often our knowledge and skill make us victorious. Sometimes, however, the sea triumphs. *Titanic* was a defeat for us, a rout really, and the stern is like the sight of one of those astounding last stands, Masada, or the Alamo, or Little Big Horn. Here, hundreds stood and died — but not for anything they believed in or anything they had done. No, they died tragically because of a mixture of institutionalized arrogance and disorganization.

At around 2:05, Captain Smith entered the wireless shack and told Phillips and Bride, "You can do no more. Now it's every man for himself." Forward of the Marconi Room, Lightoller and others were struggling to get Collapsible B down from the roof of the officers' quarters on the port side; on the other side of the first funnel, Murdoch and a small group were trying to do the same with Collapsible A. They tried to slide it down to the boat deck on a pile of oars, but they splintered under the weight of the boat.

One of the first accounts written of the sinking was by Colonel Archibald Gracie, an American amateur historian whose book, *The Truth About the Titanic,* was published in 1913. Gracie and his pal Clinch Smith watched as Lightoller and others struggled to get the collapsible off the roof. Then, seeing water hitting the bridge and gurgling up through nearby openings, they figured that the collapsible would never be launched in time. Instead, they decided to take their chances by heading to the stern.

"We had taken but a few steps in the direction," Gracie wrote, "when there arose before us from the decks below, a mass of humanity several lines deep, covering the Boat Deck, facing us, and completely blocking our passage toward the stern." They seemed to be steerage passengers only now making their way to the deck, and many of them, he reported, were women. On seeing the wave of

The stern of *Titanic* today.

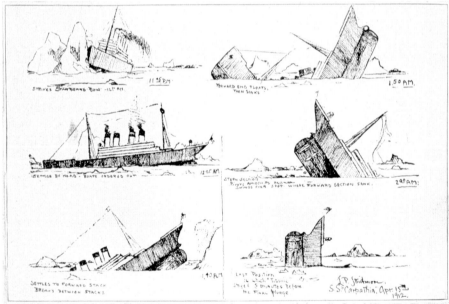

Above: Survivor Jack Thayer, who spent the night on a capsized lifeboat, described the sinking of the *Titanic* to a passenger on the *Carpathia*, who created this diagram. Thayer claimed the ship broke in two, something some experts disputed — and which turned out to be correct.

Left: As the bow slipped ever lower and the water crept up her decks, more and more people crowded toward the ship's stern. The boats were gone and there was no escape. All they could do was work their way back, hanging on as the angle of the doomed liner increased.

Opposite: Collapsible B upside down in the water. Swept off the deck when the *Titanic* began her final plunge, twenty-eight men survived a frigid night standing on its hull in soaking wet clothing.

water racing up the deck, they turned and, like Gracie and his friend, began heading for the stern. Gracie himself managed to get onto the top of the cabin and survived. His friend Smith did not.

Titanic's stern rose higher and higher into the air. The crowds of people continued to struggle, many sliding down the deck and into the onrushing water. Others grabbed ventilators and benches and held on for all they were worth. The air was filled with the sound of tearing metal, as boilers and machinery inside the ship began to slide forward, ripping out the bulkheads between compartments. The forward funnel dropped into the sea with a shower of sparks and soot, washing Collapsible B off the deck of the ship. Then the lights, which had stayed on throughout the sinking thanks to the ship's engineers, went out. (The engineers had virtually guaranteed their deaths by staying at their posts.) The ship began to split between the third and fourth funnels. The forward part of the ship slid away. Her stern seemed to slowly settle back to almost an even keel. Then, after a moment, the shattered forward section disappeared below the surface, the stern again rising into the air until it was virtually vertical. At this, the stern began to sink, picking up speed as it did. One of the few survivors from the stern, Chief Baker Charles Joughin, who would survive two hours in the sea that night thanks to the amount of whiskey he had drunk, likened it to an elevator going down — at the end he simply stepped off the stern.

Soon, the lucky few who had made it into the boats were treated to the horrific cries of those from the stern as they struggled in the freezing water. It was 2:20 a.m. — two hours and thirty minutes since the iceberg had been spotted. Seven hundred and five had been saved; more than fifteen hundred had died.

CHAPTER FIVE

FINDING THE TITANIC

IN THE AFTERMATH of the sinking, White Star chartered a number of ships working out of Halifax, Nova Scotia, to search for the bodies of those who had died. First to leave port was a cable-laying ship named the *Mackay-Bennett*, which managed to recover 306 bodies, including that of John Jacob Astor, who was found with more than 2,500 dollars on his person. The ship kept only those bodies that could be identified or were in good enough condition to be embalmed; the others were buried at sea. After a week, *Mackay-Bennett* headed for Halifax with 190 bodies onboard, the first-class victims in coffins on the deck, second-class, third-class, and crew sewn into canvas shrouds and stowed in ice in the hold. In death, as in life, it seemed the nuances of *Titanic*'s class divisions still held sway. Three other ships followed *Mackay-Bennett* in her grim business. Due to ocean currents, winds, and worsening weather, only an additional eighteen bodies were recovered before the search was called off.

As well as their grim human cargo, the recovery vessels picked up various pieces of wooden wreckage. There was a panel that came from the first-class lounge and the carved facing from a newel post on one of the first-class staircases. The searchers also found a teak deck chair, one of hundreds that had been onboard and were tossed over the side that night as makeshift life rafts.

Debris from *Titanic*. Early ideas about salvaging the ship began to emerge within weeks of her sinking. It was assumed that somewhere down there (and no one was certain quite where *there* was) the ship was sitting upright and intact.

For many years, that deck chair could boast an odd distinction (well, it shared it with another deck chair). As the sun rose on April 15, 1912, the survivors slowly made their way toward the Cunard liner *Carpathia*, under Captain Arthur Rostron, who had steamed at record speed through the ice field after receiving *Titanic*'s distress call. One by one, the boats came alongside and unloaded their passengers, including J. Bruce Ismay, who was led away to the doctor's cabin and seems to have suffered some sort of breakdown. Thirteen of *Titanic*'s lifeboats were hauled aboard *Carpathia*, and later unloaded at the White Star dock in New York. A day or two later, workmen unscrewed the White Star symbols and *Titanic* nameplates from the boats and they quickly vanished into history. White Star may have shipped them back to England and hastily added them to *Olympic*'s complement of boats, but no one is really sure. With their disappearance, that deck chair became the largest artifact in existence with a connection to the lost liner. All that was left were some wooden remnants, the odd life jacket and a few small odds and ends.

And yet, it seemed as if people couldn't let her rest. Within hours of the last boat being hauled aboard *Carpathia*, people were talking about bringing the ship up. Vincent Astor, son of John Jacob, seems to have been the first to suggest it, before his father's body was in fact discovered. Later that year, the Wideners and the Guggenheims joined with the Astor family and contacted the Merritt and Chapman Wrecking Company to talk about the (technically impossible) task of salvaging the ship. Two years later, *Popular Mechanics,* in a piece on underwater photography, speculated that someday the children of those who died might see photos of the wreck.

Above: An illustration from the December 1981 issue of *National Geographic* showing how the *Argo/Jason* system I was working on would explore the floor of the ocean.
Right: Me with Woods Hole scientist Dr. Wilfred B. Bryan aboard the ship *Lucy* during Project Famous, 1974.

Like the general wave of interest in the ship that hit in the relatively short months after the sinking, interest in raising *Titanic* waned with the outbreak of the First World War. It resurfaced, with the same buoyancy that enthusiasts hoped the ship would, as the interest in things *Titanic* took off again in the 1950s. Looking at some of these ideas, it quickly becomes clear that any lessons the ship's tragedy might have taught us about making a false god of technology had not been absorbed. One scheme called for the ship to be pumped full of Ping-Pong balls, ignoring the fact that at *Titanic*'s depth, 12,500 feet, they would have been crushed flat. Another equally impractical idea was to attach enormous pontoons to the hull which, when filled with helium or gasoline, would raise the ship. If nothing else, it creates a lovely image of the battered liner slowly rising through the dappled light of the sea (perhaps to the music of Strauss). And if that didn't work, someone else had suggested a submarine equipped with an electro-magnet.

There was just something about the idea that people couldn't leave alone. Clive Cussler even wrote a best-selling novel about it, *Raise the* Titanic (it was later made into a high-budget fiasco by British mogul Lew Grade, who joked that it would probably be cheaper to lower the Atlantic). All these schemes, of course, tended to gloss over one minor problem: *Titanic* had to first be found. The ship's general location was known (the distress call that night had given it as 41 46' N, 50 14' W), but that still left a lot of ocean — make that very deep ocean — to look at.

When I look at it now, the diagram has a slightly dated look, the colors a little jarring to my eyes. It's a bit like a cover for *Analog* or *Amazing Stories*, one of those pulp science fiction magazines from my teens, the ones that used to publish the work of Arthur C. Clarke and Isaac Asimov. What it showed did not yet exist, but it was not fantasy. First published in *National Geographic* in December 1981, it illustrated the basic workings of my *Argo/Jason* system developed when I was a youngish scientist at the Woods Hole Oceanographic

Institution. *Argo* was the box-like contraption seen here (people often compared it to a sled), which was connected directly to the surface ship. The way I thought of it, the surface ship would first scan the bottom by sonar, creating a three-dimensional map of the area. *Argo* would be equipped with two sonar systems, one checking ahead for obstacles and a side-scanning sonar to investigate the bottom, along with several cameras that would give operators on the surface a view of the sea floor. *Jason* would come into play whenever they spotted anything interesting. Carried in a housing aboard *Argo* and tethered to it by a cable, the small craft would boast thrusters to let it move up and down, its own cameras and lights, and arms or "manipulators" to gather samples.

I had been aware of the *Titanic* story for many years (you couldn't be as interested in what was under the sea as I had been since my teens and not know about it). But when I first hatched the idea of finding the ship, back in 1973, my real goal was to demonstrate the usefulness of the undersea exploration equipment I was already thinking about. Over the years, though, finding the ship become a bit of a personal obsession. Especially after I met the late William H. Tantum IV. Bill, a member of the *Titanic* Historical Society, was popularly known as "Mr. Titanic," and he seemed to know everything there was to know about the ship. It was thanks to Bill that I really came to understand the human story at the heart of *Titanic*, and acquire some of his passion for the ship. Bill didn't live to see my triumph (he died in 1980), but he never stopped believing.

And there would be plenty of time when I would need his faith. The same year I met Bill, 1977, I had my first crack at really finding *Titanic*, using the *Alcoa Seaprobe*. Essentially a drilling ship adopted for deep-sea research, the *Alcoa Seaprobe* was equipped with a derrick and thousands of feet of drilling pipe. Using this, I planned to lower a pod containing a sonar unit and camera to just a few feet above the ocean floor. This wasn't the kind of remotely operated vehicle that I wanted to create, but the pod would show people how my system would work when, and if, it ever came to be. Unfortu-

Left: I had originally gone looking for *Titanic* using the research ship *Alcoa Seaprobe*. Our plan was to lower a pod containing a camera and sonar at the end of thousands of feet of pipe and use it to scan the bottom.

nately, four days out on our test run, the several thousand feet of drill pipe we had lowered tore loose, burying the pod carrying my borrowed camera and sonar deep in the bottom mud. After this setback, it would be several years before I was back on the job.

In the meantime, a man called Jack Grimm began to grab headlines with his plans to find *Titanic*. A Texas oilman with a love of publicity and adventure, Grimm had previously bankrolled other ambitious expeditions, including such quixotic endeavors as looking for the Loch Ness monster and trying to locate Noah's Ark. Grimm may have been eccentric, but he wasn't stupid. To help him look, he hired two of the world's top oceanographers, Fred Spiess of the Scripps Institute and Bill Ryan from New York's Lamont-Doherty Geological Observatory. Spiess had actually turned me down for graduate work at the Scripps Institute, and we had a kind of friendly rivalry. I wanted to prove he had made the wrong decision. Now it seemed that he, Grimm, and Ryan were going to have the honor of finding *Titanic*.

Grimm's first expedition to find *Titanic* set out in July 1980, and even before it left port, the mission had problems. Grimm planned to bring along a monkey he had named Titan, which had been taught to point at the precise spot on the map where they thought *Titanic* lay. Grimm felt that Titan would spice up the movie he was planning to make of the expedition, but Spiess and Ryan were appalled. "Us or the monkey," they told Grimm. Grimm contemplated firing them, but cooler heads prevailed. Unfortunately, bad weather and technical problems hampered the mission and, at the end, *Titanic* remained unfound.

Below: After his second expedition in 1981, Texas oilman Jack Grimm (standing, left) was convinced that he and his fellow explorers had photographed *Titanic*'s propeller lying on the bottom.

Right: Grimm's chartered research vessel, *Gyre*, setting out to look for *Titanic* at the start of the 1981 expedition. Ironically enough, *Gyre*'s departure port was Woods Hole, my own home base.

For their next expedition in 1981, they returned to the area where they thought *Titanic* had sunk, equipped with a powerful side-scan sonar developed by the Scripps Institute. Working from the assumption that *Titanic* had in fact gone down farther to the east than Fourth Officer Boxhall had estimated that night (an accurate assumption as it would later turn out), Grimm and company were again unsuccessful, although they came close to finding the ship (within a mile and a half) without knowing it. While they were returning to Boston, Grimm and his researchers were viewing some color video they'd taken with a camera vehicle on their very last run when an unusual object appeared. Grimm was convinced it was *Titanic*'s propeller. Spiess and Ryan weren't so sure.

Two years later, Grimm was back at sea, steaming out from Halifax to look at his "propeller." Unfortunately rough weather dogged the trip, making a methodical search almost impossible. Grimm and his team made a few camera passes over the site. If there was a propeller down there, it certainly didn't have a ship nearby. The third time out, Grimm had not been able to raise as much money, which limited the time he could spend searching. His time up, Grimm headed for home.

During the years that Grimm had been searching for *Titanic*, I had been busy developing my ideas for the remote exploration of the seafloor. By 1984, working together with the team in the Deep Submergence Laboratory that I had created at Woods Hole, we had completed *Argo* and we were ready to test it.

One of my major financial backers for the *Argo/Jason* project was the United States Navy. And the navy, specifically Vice Admiral Ron Thurman, deputy chief of naval operations for submarine warfare, had a job for *Argo*.

In the mid-1980s, as part of the SALT (Strategic Arms Limitation Talks) with the then Soviet Union, the United States was looking at the possibility of reducing its submarine fleet. But this created a specific problem: safely disposing of the large chamber constructed especially to house the reactors on these submarines, which over time had built up low-level radiation. One suggestion was to bury them at sea. But to do this the navy had to find out what effect the radiation would have on marine life.

Nearly twenty years before, in April 1963, the American nuclear submarine *Thresher* had been lost during a test dive after a refit. In fact, the navy had found the wreckage of the *Thresher*, and then used the manned bathysphere *Trieste* to locate the reactor — unsuccessfully. The navy was worried that it could be leaking radiation. *Argo*, towed by the research ship *Knorr,* was able to photograph the scene and determine that the reactor was intact, and radiation, minimal. I made another useful discovery, one that would help me later on: the debris from the *Thresher* had spread across a wide swath of the sea bottom in a pattern that somewhat resembled a comet and its tail. The biggest wreckage from the sub formed the actual "heart" of the comet, and debris trailed away from it like a tail, the smallest, lightest pieces having been carried farthest away by the ocean currents. I realized that if you wanted to find a ship that had sunk in deep water, you didn't need to look for the ship itself. Working methodically, slowly sailing back and forth, you searched for the much larger debris trail. That would lead you to it.

But even while I was busy with navy work, I never lost sight of *Titanic*. I now had the equipment and the expertise. All I needed was the chance. Then, in 1985, we got it.

Five years after *Thresher* had been lost at sea, a second American nuclear submarine, the USS *Scorpion*, had gone to the bottom about 400 miles south of the Azores. For many years, what exactly destroyed the *Scorpion* was unclear. Like *Thresher*, *Scorpion* had been located years before, but the navy was concerned about the reactor and the fate of the two nuclear torpedoes that had been onboard. A look at the debris field might also yield clues about what had sent the sub to the bottom. The navy held out a tantalizing promise: they would underwrite three weeks' worth of investigation. If the work could be done in less time, I was free to use *Knorr* and my equipment to search for *Titanic*.

Below: The wreckage of USS *Scorpion*, photographed during one of our expeditions to the submarine for the United States Navy. The missions gave me the time and resources I needed to hunt for *Titanic*.

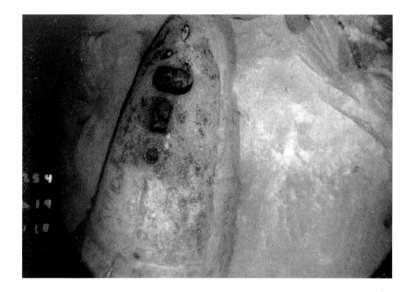

Right: Jean Louis Michel of the French oceanographic group IFERMER, photographed with the deep towed SAR sonar that we hoped would locate *Titanic*'s wreck.

Facing page: My revolu-
tionary camera sled, *Argo*,
splashes into the sea to
begin its search.

Right: After
IFERMER's SAR
sonar had failed to
find *Titanic*, it was
our turn to begin a
visual search using
Argo. By patiently
weaving back and
forth — "mowing
the lawn," as we
called it — we
hoped to spot
Titanic debris on
the bottom.

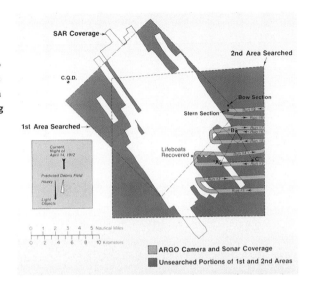

SAR Coverage

2nd Area Searched

C.Q.D.

Bow Section

Stern Section

1st Area Searched

Lifeboats
Recovered

Current,
Night of
April 14, 1912

Predicted Debris Field
Heavy

Light
Objects

0   1   2   3   4   5 Nautical Miles
0   2   4   6   8   10 Kilometers

ARGO Camera and Sonar Coverage
Unsearched Portions of 1st and 2nd Areas

Above: We celebrate
our success early on
the morning of
September 1, 1985.
Titanic had been found.

Over the years, I had worked on many projects with the French organization IFERMER (Institut Francais de Recherche pour l'Exploitation de la Mer), notably on Project Famous, the joint French-American project to explore the Mid-Atlantic Ridge. My friend Jean-Louis Michel at IFERMER had developed SAR — one of the best deep towed side-scan sonars in the world — which was ideal for locating *Titanic*'s wreck. Once I knew that I had access to *Knorr* and some time, I held out a tantalizing offer to them: help me find *Titanic*.

When it had hit the iceberg, *Titanic* had broadcast its position to any ships within range. Fourth Officer Boxhall had made the calculation using dead reckoning, starting with the ship's last known location and then extrapolating from that by factoring in the elapsed time and the ship's estimated speed. It's not a bad way of doing things and Boxhall was reputed to be a first-rate navigator, but it is inexact. Grimm had created a search area for his expeditions by taking *Titanic*'s last reported position and then trying to factor in how far she had drifted on the surface, and then under.

To determine the area we would search, we started with the location of the lifeboats when *Carpathia* had picked them up, and figured that the ship lay to the north. Then we made a few assumptions: if the ship had not been going quite as fast as Boxhall had thought, or the current was stronger than he had assumed, the ship might be even farther east than Grimm had believed. Working with these assumptions, we came up with a compact search area entirely to the east of *Titanic*'s reported sinking position.

The search for *Titanic* began in the summer of 1985. For four weeks, aboard the French research ship *Le Suroit,* under the command of Jean-Louis, we patiently "mowed" the lawn, moving back and forth across the search area, dragging IFERMER's sophisticated side-scan sonar. Hampered by strong currents and bad weather, we found nothing. On August 6, having covered seventy percent of the search area, *Le Suroit* called it quits, heading for the island of St. Pierre off Newfoundland. Jean-Louis and I jumped on the first of a series of planes that would take us south to *Knorr* in the Azores.

On August 17, having completed our survey of *Scorpion* in just four days, we steamed north in *Knorr* and resumed the search for *Titanic*. Our investigation of *Scorpion* had reinforced what we had learned from *Thresher* — on her way to the bottom, she had left that same long, comet-like trail of debris. Time was tight, and lacking the sophisticated sonar that the French had used during their portion of the search, we had no choice but to go with a visual search.

We would begin looking for a similar trail that would lead us to *Titanic*. Starting south of where *Carpathia* had picked up the ship's boats, we began working north.

For days, nonstop around the clock, we stared at mile after mile of undifferentiated brown bottom mud, *Argo* dragged ever onward by *Knorr* at a snail's pace of one knot. Morale sagged, and people began to grumble. To top it off, on August 31, the weather started getting worse. In just five days we had to head home.

That evening I had finally left the control room around midnight, just after we had changed the watch. I didn't want to go to sleep but I wanted to get away from the endless search for a while. Then shortly after midnight, the watch crew began spotting debris on the screens in the control van. Was this it? Just in case, they dispatched the ship's cook to tell me. I think I raced down three decks and ran the length of the ship in under thirty seconds. It was wreckage all right, but nothing particularly identifiable. Suddenly a round shape swam into sight. "A boiler?" someone suggested. Frantically, Jean-Louis Michel flicked through a reference book. There was an identical boiler as it had looked seventy years before awaiting installation in *Titanic*'s sister *Olympic*. Exhausted but exhilarated, I stared at the murky images on our television screens. After more than seventy-three years on the bottom, the most famous ship ever lost had been found again.

Left: The image that proved it was *Titanic*, a ghostly ship's boiler captured by *Argo* on the bottom.
Right: A similar boiler in the *Titanic* debris field photographed during our 2004 expedition.

In the few days remaining before we had to return to Woods Hole, we explored the wreck of *Titanic* using the remotely operated *Argo*, and when steadily worsening weather made operating *Argo* hazardous, we switched to ANGUS (Acoustically Navigated Geological Underwater Survey), affectionately known as "Dope on a Rope." Using ANGUS, we snapped hundreds of underwater photographs of the ship.

We returned to a hero's welcome in Woods Hole on September 9, 1985, and newspapers and television news programs around the world featured ghostly pictures of the wreck. Unfortunately, misunderstandings about how the news was to be released, and by whom, led to a falling out between us and our French colleagues.

As a result, in July 1986, when we returned to *Titanic*, it was without the help of IFERMER. This year, I brought the miniature submersible *Alvin* plus my remotely operated vehicle *Jason, Jr.*, which would be carried by *Alvin* and used as a sort of roving eyeball to explore *Titanic* more closely — perhaps even going inside the wreck. (As in 1985, part of my work that summer involved examining the wrecks of *Thresher* and *Scorpion* for the navy, using *Jason, Jr.* to examine their reactors and nuclear weapons. We looked for but found no signs of radioactive leakage.)

We arrived at the *Titanic* sinking site onboard *Atlantis II* on July 12, 1986. Over the course of the next twelve days, we made ten dives, crammed inside *Alvin*'s tiny crew compartment. Because it took so long to reach the wreck then return to the surface (at its fastest, *Alvin* could rise at a rate of only 100 feet a minute), our exploration time at the ship was limited. As well, the great depths and the delicacy of our equipment often meant either *Alvin* or *Jason, Jr.* were not operating properly. Despite these obstacles, we managed to explore a good deal of the two sections of the wreck and the debris field. We even sent *Jason, Jr.* deep inside the ship via the first-class staircase.

In the years since, a lot of other expeditions have visited the ship, starting with IFERMER in 1987. The ship has been visited by various film crews (including director James Cameron who first

Facing page: *Jason, Jr.* photographed from *Alvin* in 1986. I returned to the *Titanic* wreck site in July 1986, equipped with the submersible *Alvin* and my remotely operated vehicle *Jason, Jr.*

Below: Over the course of twelve days, we made ten dives on the wreck, photographing the ship extensively, landing on its decks and even sending *Jason, Jr.* down into the ship via the first-class staircase.

Bottom: *Alvin* carried on the gantry mounted on the stern of *Atlantis II.*

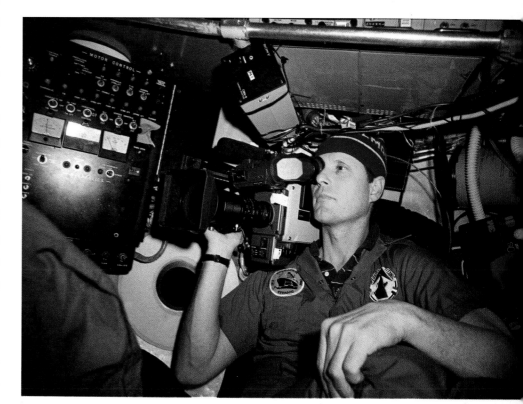

Left: After my trip to *Titanic* in 1986, I was uncertain if I would ever return. I finally did in 2004, equipped with new remotely operated vehicles and digital cameras.

Below: Since my 1986 expedition, numerous others have visited *Titanic* to explore, to film, or to lift souvenirs. Film director James Cameron visited the ship before making

his blockbuster, again in 2001 to make the documentary *Titanic: Ghosts of the Abyss*, and most recently in 2004. Overleaf: *Hercules* explores *Titanic*'s promenade deck.

visited it in 1995, again in 2001, and just after us in 2004, although his last trip was beset with technical problems). Probably the strangest visitors of all were the couple who were actually married aboard a small submersible perched on *Titanic*. A company called RMS Titanic, which claims salvage rights to the ship, has removed thousands of objects from the debris field.

Some expeditions have been careful; others have not. But the long-term effect of all these visits to the wreck has been to speed up the ship's natural decay.

When I left *Titanic* in 1986, I wasn't certain if I would ever return. I did, of course, in 2004. Will I ever go back again? Sure, I wouldn't mind going back in another twenty years to see how she's doing. I'll be eighty-five, but I plan to still be around.

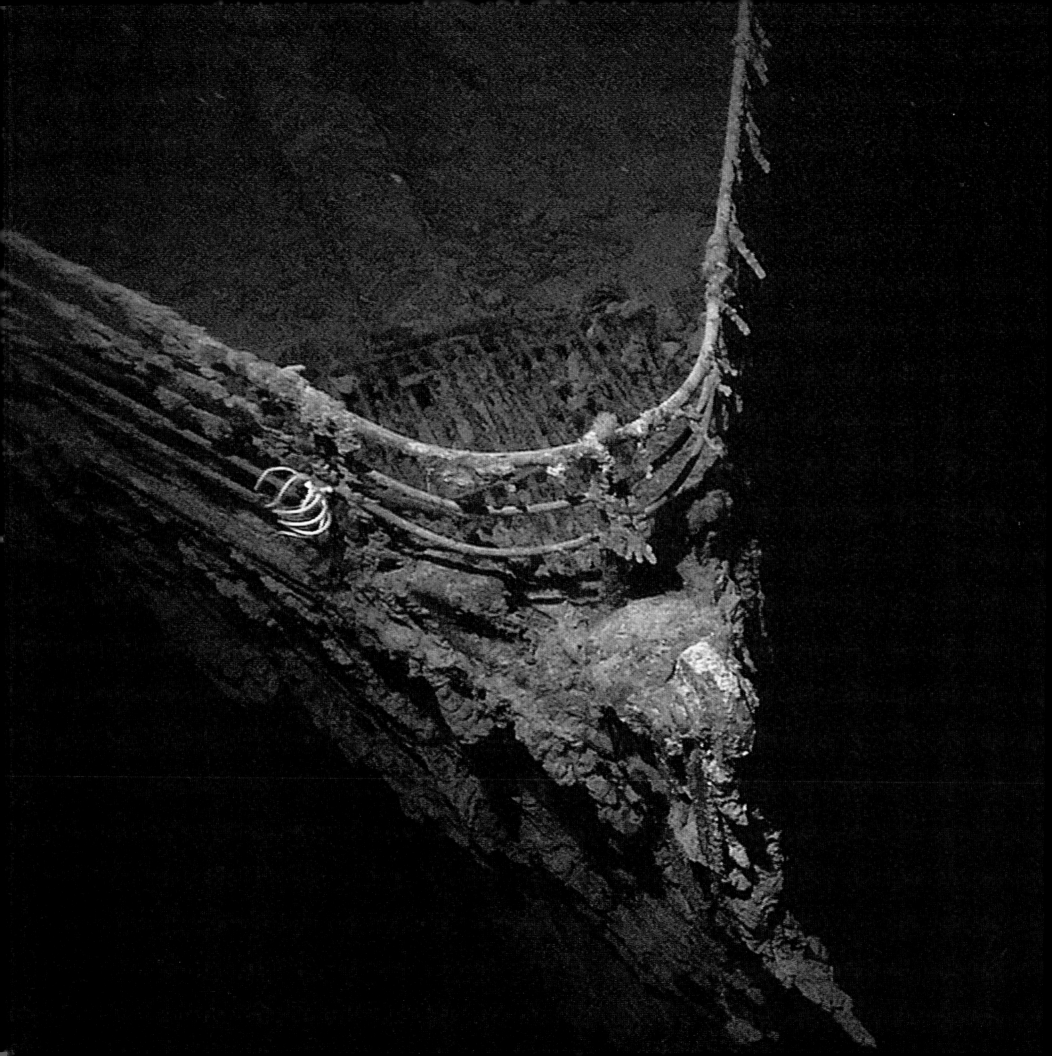

CHAPTER SIX

TOURING THE TITANIC MUSEUM

ELSEWHERE WE HAVE LOOKED at separate parts of the ship as they related to different parts of the story. In chapter six, we are going to put the ship together. Let's start at the beginning, the bow, work our way along the forward part of the ship, and then visit the debris field. After that, we'll move on to the stern, touring the ship as though it's a museum. Except we're not just learning about the sinking or how the ship was built. It's the whole museum we're interested in touring. We'll do it the way a tourist would the Louvre.

Of course, you don't just want to wander into a museum on your own. You need a guide. Well, in this case we are going to have three: Jeremy Weirich of the NOAA, who was the underwater archeologist on our 2004 expedition; Dr. Dwight Coleman, an oceanographer with the University of Rhode Island, who is also on staff at the Institute for Exploration at Mystic Museum; and, finally, me, Dr. Robert Ballard, the original discoverer of *Titanic*, and the father, I guess you could say, of telepresence, the revolutionary system for exploring the ocean depths. We're going to talk about what you're seeing and, I think, give you another perspective on it.

The doors are open; let's go in.

Titanic today. "In a solitude of the sea/Deep from human vanity/And the Pride of Life that planned her/stilly couches she." —Thomas Hardy.

Your Guide to the Museum

One of the goals of the 2004 expedition was to take photographs to create a new digital mosaic that would help scientists evaluate the ship's condition. Comparing it to the original mosaic, on page 30–31, is illuminating. Overall, *Titanic* still looks the same, but the new high-definition images used to create the mosaic help us pick out disturbing changes: orange blooms of rust forward, the missing crow's nest down in the well deck, and numerous holes in the steel around the skylight to the Marconi Room, just aft of the expansion joint. If nothing is done, the deterioration will only continue.

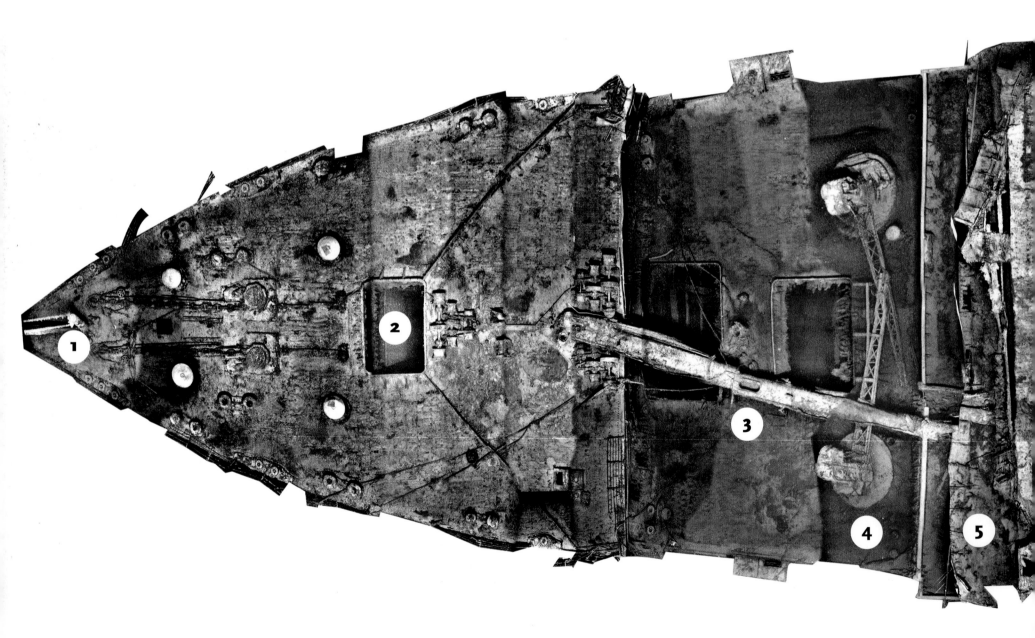

Key to Modern Mosaic of *Titanic*

1 Anchor crane.

2 Number 1 hatch.

3 Opening in mast for missing crow's nest.

4 Forward cargo cranes.

5 Promenade deck.

6 Telemotor.

7 Welin davit on deck.

8 Davit for No.2 boat.

9 Captain's quarters.

10 Opening for first funnel.

11 Forward expansion joint.

12 Marconi Room skylight and area of deck damage.

13 First-class staircase.

14 Davit for No. 8 boat.

15 Opening for second funnel.

16 Gymnasium.

THE BOW

ROBERT BALLARD: The ship sits well down in the mud today. When we first came in on the bow back in 1986, we could almost see this bow wake of mud, and the impression you got was that *Titanic* was still plowing ahead, trying to get to New York. I almost felt like I had to jump aside because it was going to run me over.

Left: The ship sits considerably deeper in the mud than she did originally in the water. As a result, the starboard anchor today is just a few feet above the sea bottom.

Left: *Titanic*'s portside anchor is covered in weeping rust.

Right: The ROV *Hercules* closes in on the small crane on *Titanic*'s bow. Located just above the ship's port and starboard anchors, it was intended for lifting the ship's auxiliary anchor overboard if needed.

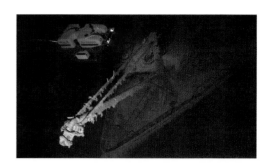

THE BOW

BALLARD: The very bow of the ship [previous page] hasn't changed much. When you see it, you naturally think of the Leonardo DiCaprio scene in the *Titanic* movie with Kate Winslett: "I'm the king of the world." That was something you had to chuckle about. This area was off limits to passengers. They would never let anyone up there.

When you move farther back on the bow, there seems to be a lot of railings knocked down. I am sure that's due to submarine collisions. In fact, look at the little crane just forward of here and you'll see a smack mark where they clearly hit it.

Previous page: Titanic's bow today is a spot well known to fans of James Cameron's *Titanic*.

Bottom: The port side of *Titanic* forward, showing two bollards and a section of damaged railing.

Right: *Titanic*'s massive anchor chains flank a small hatch.

THE NUMBER ONE HATCH

DWIGHT COLEMAN: We used two ROVs, *Argus* and *Hercules*. They are both equipped with cameras and lights, but since *Argus* has the more powerful lights, we used it to illuminate a much larger area and keep an eye on *Hercules*.

Above: A heavy duty steam winch located just aft of the number one hold.

Right: *Titanic*'s number one hatch illuminated here by *Argus*. One of two used to load the ship's cargo (which included a brand new Renault automobile, rough oak beams, and ostrich plumes), this hatch is located on the raised forecastle deck forward.

THE WELL DECK

BALLARD: To me, the cutest thing was that yellow radiator. It just floated down after the ship sank. The bow was the heaviest part of the ship and it hit bottom first. Moments later that heater probably came clunking down and landed there.

WEIRICH: That was something that hadn't been seen before. It had been passed over. *Hercules* has thrusters set at different angles and a special navigation system that helps it stay in place by thrusting in different directions. It can hold position to a tenth of a meter, which is pretty amazing. Because it can hold station, we could take a really good look at some of these details and then zoom right in.

Below: One of *Titanic*'s small electric heaters now nestled in the forward portion of the ship's well deck. These heaters were located throughout the liner, and this one would have fallen free when the ship broke in two.

Left: *Hercules* also photographed this valve in the well deck, just forward of where *Titanic*'s foremast once stood. Its operating instructions are still visible on the small central hub.

THE FOREMAST

BALLARD: The sad part is the missing crow's nest. Someone knocked it off. I won't say who, but in one of those expeditions to the wreck, at one point, if you watch their documentary, they show the crow's nest intact, and then later they show it missing. They don't say anything, but isn't it odd that during one dive it's there, and then it's not?

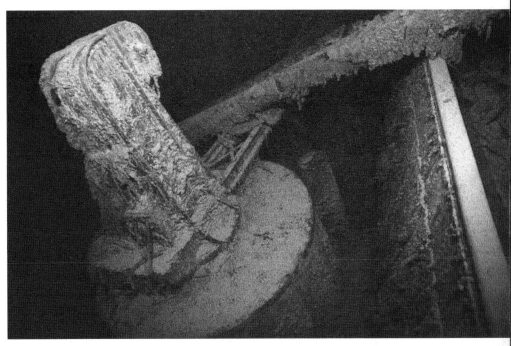

Left: *Titanic*'s foremast was knocked back into the forward super-structure, probably by the force of the water as the ship sank. The mast broke where it hit the forward railing of the promenade deck, flattening it.

Above: The base of one of *Titanic*'s two forward cargo cranes, with the mast visible behind.

Overleaf: The rushing water also tore off the wheelhouse and seems to have peeled back the superstructure. Virtually nothing of the bridge remains. The surviving davit for the No. 2 boat is visible here in the foreground.

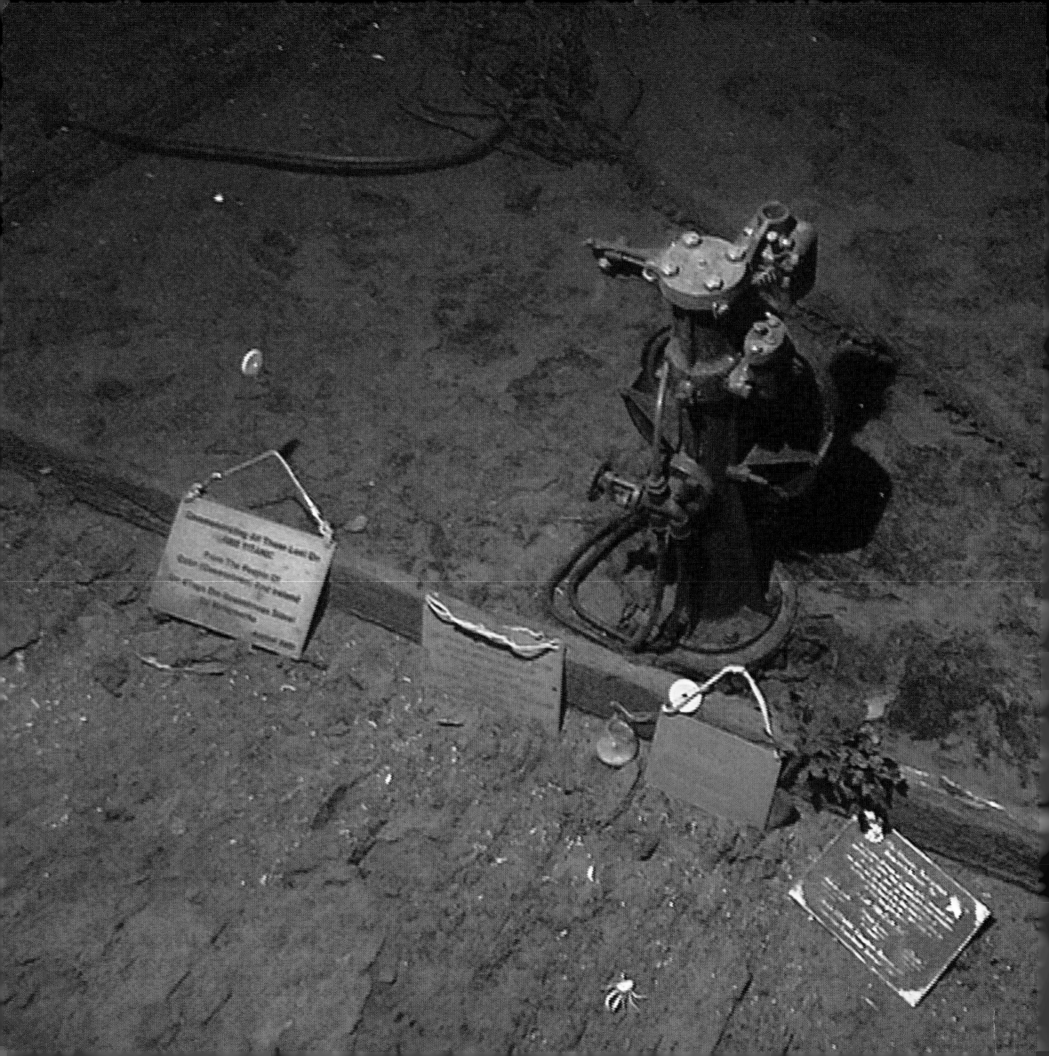

THE BRIDGE

BALLARD: Leaving these plaques has become part of the ritual for anyone visiting *Titanic*, but we've stopped leaving things. We don't land; we don't touch. We're learning the damage it can cause. Someone took the plaque we left on the bow back in 1986, so we left a replacement, but down on the bottom near the bow. I don't want to say exactly where because someone will take it.

Opposite: Plaques left on the wreck rest against the base of the long-vanished wheelhouse. Among those left on the ship are (left) one in memory of the five postal workers who perished aboard *Titanic*, (middle) one laid on behalf of the British *Titanic* Society and (bottom) a third left behind by the IMAX-*Titanic* joint Canadian, Russian and American expedition of 1991.

Overleaf: This section of the promenade deck just below the bridge shows advanced deterioration.

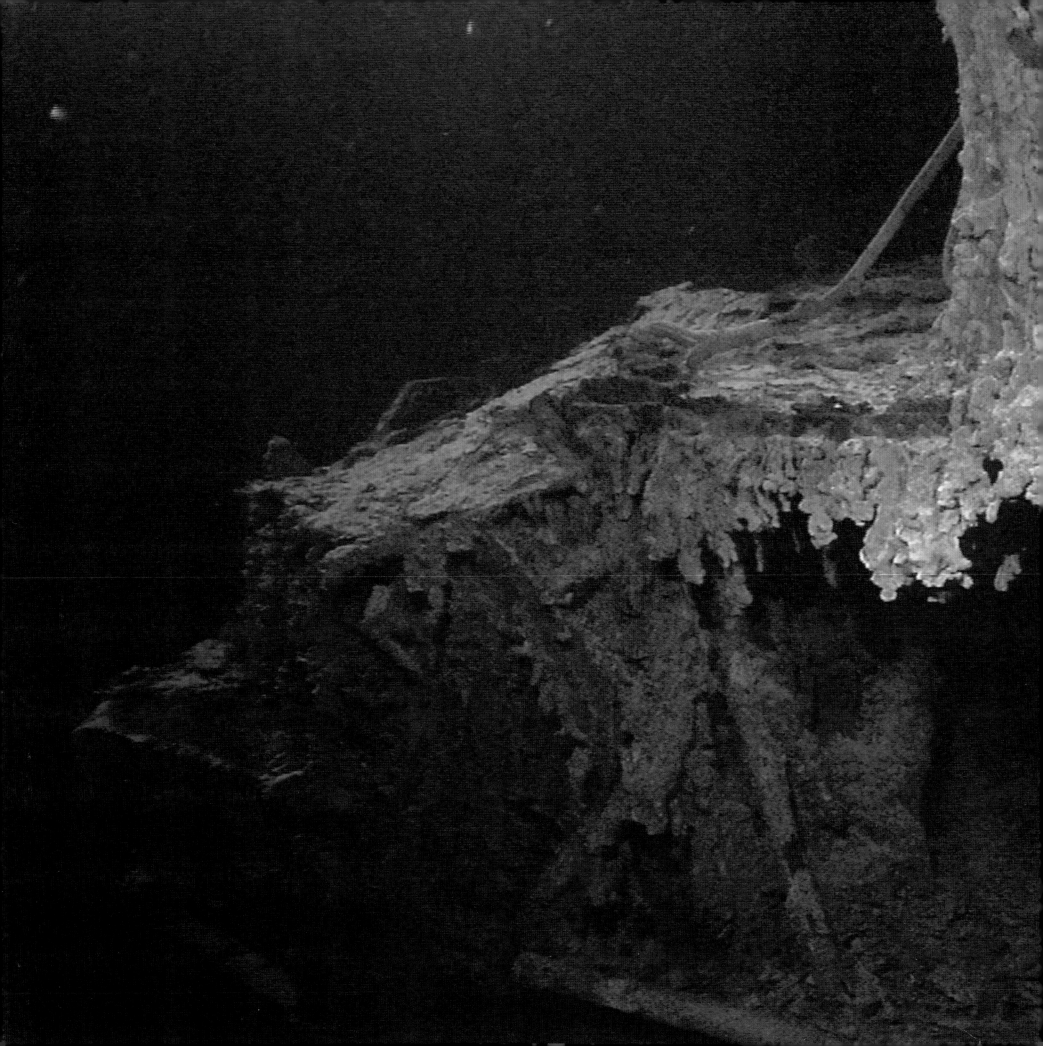

The Officers' Quarters

BALLARD: There's a little sign there, and you can actually read it. The one thing I found that we could do on this trip that we could never do before was zoom in and read things. This or the name of manufacturers on different pieces of equipment. On the cranes there were all sorts of instructions, and we zoomed in and read about how to operate them.

COLEMAN: For me, this part of the ship — the bridge deck, the telemotor, the davits that held the lifeboats — really brings out the human element. You start getting the feeling that, my God, fifteen hundred people died.

Previous page: The location of the number one funnel, as seen from where Collapsible A was stored on the roof of the officers' quarters.

Left: The large curved vent and the round ventilator are just behind where the first funnel once stood. The small opening to the right of the round vent was the skylight for the officers' washroom.

Above: The sign announcing "OFFICERS' ENTRANCE" outside their quarters on the boat deck is visible just behind a rusticle.

CAPTAIN SMITH'S QUARTERS

WEIRICH: The bulkhead's gone here, and you can zoom in and actually see the faucets and the piping. That was Captain Smith's bathtub.

BALLARD: That bulkhead was upright in 1986. Some people would say that it's natural decay. Is it? It's almost impossible to say for sure, but to me it's clear that the damage here has been accelerated by human activity.

Right: *Hercules* examining the captain's quarters close up.

Left: This rusting rubble is all that remains of the captain's bedroom. Below: The captain's bath seen through the now decayed bulkhead, the still-white tub filled with rust.

THE FORWARD EXPANSION JOINT

WEIRICH: *Titanic* had two expansion joints. This is the forward one, right after the first stack, up near the officers' quarters. It was probably the impact with the bottom that opened it up. There's still a whole lot to be learned from *Titanic*. For my purposes as an underwater archeologist, looking at *Titanic* will teach us how other steel wrecks will be affected over time.

Left: The expansion joint continues down through the promenade deck. Below and right: *Titanic*'s superstructure just forward of the expansion joint shows some signs of severe bending, perhaps caused when the ship hit bottom. The expansion joint ran through one of the officers' washrooms, and a sink can be made out just on the right of the joint.

STATEROOM WINDOW (PAGES 154–155)

COLEMAN: The staterooms had windows that opened out like this. This is one of them with the window frame intact, and even the glass still there. It is pretty amazing to think that this ship sank more than 2 miles and then hit bottom and the glass didn't break.

MARCONI ROOM (PAGES 156–157)

WEIRICH: The submersibles that have visited the ship have landed primarily in two places: up forward and here on top of the Marconi Room. From here they could look down the void that used to be the grand staircase. They can generally control their buoyancy, so they don't put weight on the deck. But they still rubbed up against the steel, causing deterioration.

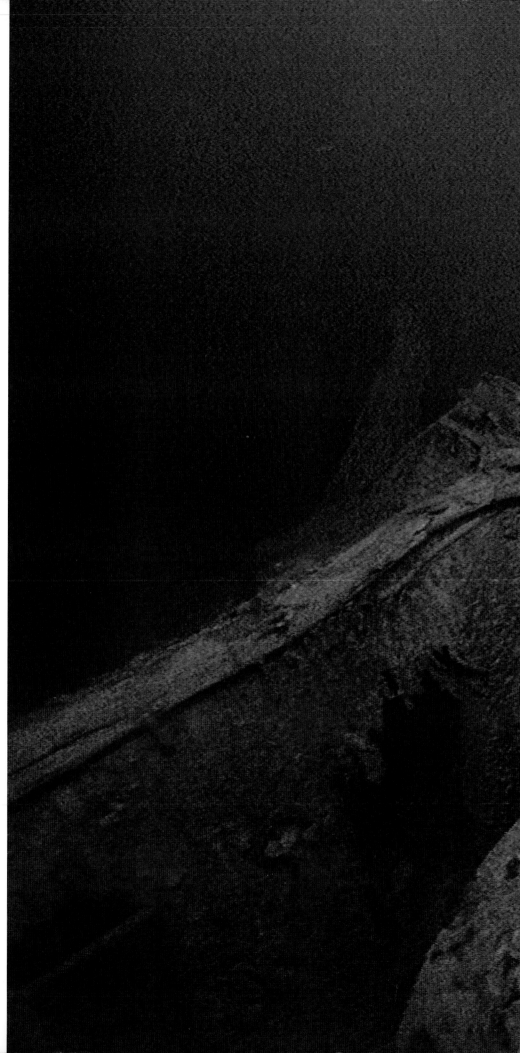

Above: This ventilator located on the roof of the first-class lounge is not far forward from where the ship broke in two.

Right: Just aft of the first-class staircase on the port side.

Below: This hole in
Titanic's deck was
visible back in 1986,
but it has increased in
size in the ensuing
twenty years.

Left: This electric motor,
used to raise the boats,
was located just forward
of the first-class staircase.

Right: The entrance to
the first-class stairway
on the port side of
the ship.

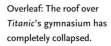

Overleaf: The roof over
Titanic's gymnasium has
completely collapsed.

Debris field

Ballard: The debris field has been picked over, but there are virgin areas because it is impossible to see it all. I was so glad to see how much the souvenir hunters didn't get — although I hope that doesn't encourage them to go back.

Coleman: Our philosophy is to preserve and protect the ship as a museum. We're not learning anything more by recovering artifacts, so let's just leave everything in place. Visit it with video cameras, but don't touch anything.

Left: A fragment of *Titanic*'s hull, broken off when the ship split in two. Below: Behind this metal bench end sits a piece of modern debris — a plastic cup dropped from the surface.

Right: Other recognizable objects in the debris field include a leather suitcase. Overleaf: A comb, a mirror, a woman's shoes and smaller shoes — perhaps a little girl's.

THE DEBRIS FIELD

WEIRICH: Looking at the debris field, it's striking what's been left behind by missions after Bob discovered *Titanic*. There are huge chandeliers down there to light areas for film expeditions. The stern section is a tangle of polypropylene, and there are chains left from when they were trying to lift up items.

Left, above and top:
Chains and sand bags,
probably used as ballast
to drag gasoline-filled
balloons to the bottom
in the August 1996
attempt to raise a
section of the hull.

Previous page: The
controls for one of the
aft cargo cranes now sit
in *Titanic*'s debris field.

THE STERN

BALLARD: It's a battered mess, but there's a lot more to the stern than you think. You can see the fallen aft mast, and you can make out windows, too. But people don't visit it much. You look at the bow and remember the ship afloat; you look at the stern and think of the disaster. It's the last retreat, where everyone leaped to their deaths.

Previous page: Much of the ship's stern has been so badly damaged as to be unrecognizable. Left: Fairlead rollers for handling lines are visible on the stern.

Left: Elsewhere, decks have been flipped right over, although some details such as (middle) these square ports and (right) this skylight can be made out.
Bottom: The main mast lies across the deck.

Below it can be seen a spittoon that floated down after the stern hit bottom.
Overleaf: Square ports, located somewhere in second class, can be seen under overhanging wreckage.

FAREWELL TITANIC

APRIL 14, 2062. INTEREST HAS BEEN building for days, but now, as the actual hour approaches, activity on the site is off the map. Everywhere, people seem to have the same idea: visit the *Titanic* undersea museum one hundred and fifty years to the very moment that she went down. Most people will be disappointed, but if they wait, and are patient, they will still get their chance before long to take a look at *Titanic*, even to travel through it, by clicking rollovers on a diagram of the ship. They will tour the first-class dining room — what's left of it — see where Captain Smith stood when he learned the ship was doomed, and look down the length of the ruined, ghostly promenade deck. There are many famous ships in the world that you can visit, physically or remotely — Nelson's flagship HMS *Victory*, or the USS *Constitution*, "Old Ironsides." There are even great lost ships that have been raised from the bottom and installed in special museums, Sweden's *Vasa*, or England's famed *Mary Rose*. But now, when even the grandchildren of every survivor are gone and transatlantic sea travel is distant history, *Titanic* remains the most famous lost ship of all time.

It's a wonderful dream, and one that any fan of the ship might hope would come true, not just because we might like to really explore the ship ourselves, for many of us may not be around to see that, but because we want others to be able to experience her.

But what if the dream never comes true? What then? Suppose that the ship just slowly crumbles? The actual disaster was a long

Looking down the opening for *Titanic*'s forwardmost funnel.

time ago. We don't really remember it; what we know is what we have seen and read about it. And that record is from other people's memories, works based on what eyewitnesses such as Jack Thayer, Colonel Gracie, and Lawrence Beesley recorded not long after the sinking, or writers such as Walter Lord were able to gather from the survivors while they were still alive. Every repetition takes us farther away, is a copy of a copy of a copy. By focusing on the wreck of *Titanic*, this book has tried to get beyond that, to serve up the story fresh. But if the wreck vanishes forever, what will people do? Will anyone even care when the 150th anniversary rolls around?

Yes, they will. And people will still be discovering the ship and falling in love with it and its saga. Ultimately, all the books and films, even the magnificent, mistreated ruin on the bottom are a bit like the debris trail that we spotted that led us to the liner in the first place back in 1985. What grabs us, ultimately, is not this book or that movie, but this incredible human story and the emotions that go with it. That's what I learned from Bill Tantum. And the interesting thing about *Titanic* is that you can study the story for years, learn all the facts, have it down cold, and yet still find that, every once in a while, it's hitting you all over again. Why weren't there enough lifeboats? Why didn't they slow down? What did they feel?

That isn't going to go away, and people will continue to be led to the story. On a rainy afternoon, someone is going to find a decaying copy of Walter Lord's *A Night to Remember* on the shelves and start reading. In a hotel room somewhere, a man who can't sleep is going to flick on the television at one in the morning and be drawn into James Cameron's epic. After singing about it around the campfire, a little girl is going to start wondering why, exactly, husbands and wives and children lost their lives.

Books and films may come and go; even wrecks can disappear. They just get us started. What we seek is the human story at the heart of *Titanic*.

That will never perish.

Left: Given enough time, even the most durable remnants of the ship, like these shoes and this china, will fade away.
Pages 184-185: This open stateroom window was unchanged from when we photographed twenty years before.
Overleaf: Our memorial plaque. But what will not disappear is the human story, the fact that, on its maiden voyage, on this ship, long ago, 1,500 people lost their lives.

IN MEMORY OF THOSE
WITH THE "TITANIC"
DEDICATED TO
WHOSE DREAM TO FIND
BEEN REALIZED BY DR.
THE OFFICERS AND
TITANIC HISTORICAL

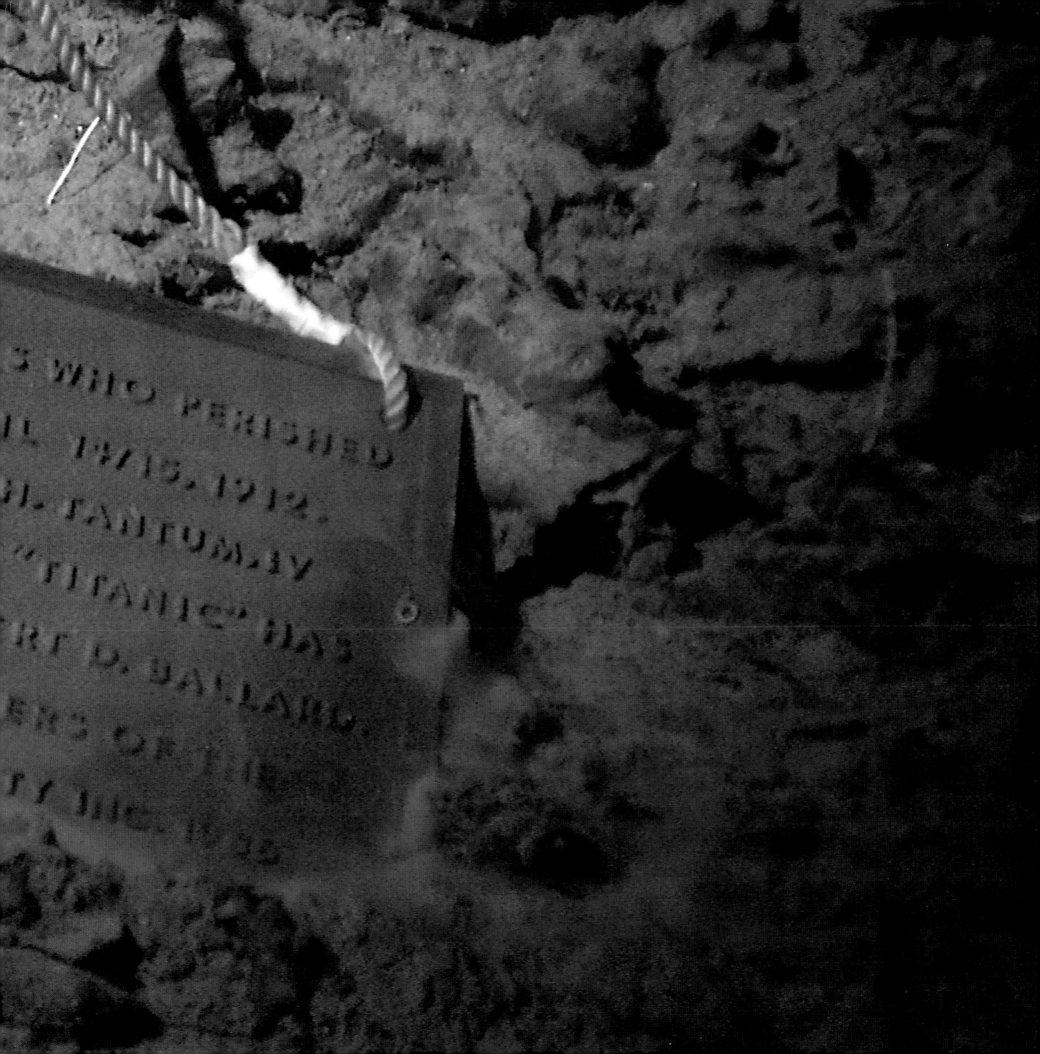

PHOTOGRAPH AND ILLUSTRATION CREDITS

Every effort has been made to correctly attribute all material reproduced in this book. If any errors have unwittingly occurred, we will be happy to correct them in future editions.

BB – Brown Brothers
FBC – Father Browne SJ Collection
IFE/IAO – Institute for Exploration/Institute for Archaeological Oceanography – University of Rhode Island
ILN – *Illustrated London News*
MM – Mariners' Museum
MPC – Madison Press Collection
NG – National Geographic
NMM – National Maritime Museum
NSARM – Nova Scotia Archives and Record Management
THS – *Titanic* Historical Society
UFT – Ulster Folk and Transport Museum
WHOI – Woods Hole Oceanographic Institution

1 IFE/IAO
2 IFE/IAO
6–7 IFE/IAO
8–9 IFE/IAO

Introduction
10–11 IFE/IAO
12 All photos IFE/IAO
13 IFE/IAO
14–15 IFE/IAO
16–17 IFE/IAO
18 NG
19 (Top) NG; (Bottom) IFE/IAO
20–21 IFE/IAO

Chapter One
22–23 IFE/IAO
24 UFT
25 (Top) UFT; (Bottom) UFT
26 UFT
27 (Top) ILN; (Bottom) Parks Stephenson Collection
28 Getty/Hulton Archive
29 (Top) THS (Bottom) Getty
30–31 WHOI
32–33 IFE/IAO
36–37 IFE/IAO

Chapter Two
38–39 IFE/IAO
40 (Top) NMM; (Bottom) UFT

41 (Top) Getty; (Bottom) THS
42 (Top) Eric Sauder Collection; (Bottom) NMM
43 (Top) UFT; (Bottom) MM
44–45 IFE/IAO
46 UFT
47 UFT
48 Photo courtesy of Jeremy Nightingale
49 Both photos IFE/IAO
50 (Top) Simon Mills Collection; (Bottom) MM
51 MPC

Chapter Three
52–53 IFE/IAO
54–55 All photos IFE/IAO
56–57 IFE/IAO
57 Both photos Library of Congress
58–59 IFE/IAO
60 FBC
61 UFT
62 MPC
63 (Top) FBC; (Bottom) BB
64 (Top) Photo courtesy of Jeremy Nightingale; (Bottom left) MPC; (Bottom right) MPC
65 (Top) Corbis/Bettmann Archive; (Bottom) FBC
66–67 IFE/IAO
68 (Top) ILN; (Middle) MPC; (Bottom) NMM
69 NMM
70–71 IFE/IAO
72–73 All photos IFE/IAO
75 Photo courtesy of Jeremy Nightingale

Chapter Four
76–77 IFE/IAO
78–79 IFE/IAO
80 (Top) MPC; (Middle) WHOI; (Bottom) BB
81 UFT
82 IFE/IAO
83 (Top) FBC; (Bottom left) Marconi Company Limited; (Bottom right) ILN
84 (Top) British Newspaper Library; (Bottom) THS
85 ILN
86–87 IFE/IAO
87 Bill Sauder Collection
88 MPC
89 (Top) *The Shipbuilder;* (Middle) Getty/ Hulton Archive; (Bottom) FBC
90–91 IFE/IAO
92–93 IFE/IAO
94 Collection of George Behe
95 (Top) *Cork Examiner;* (Bottom) ILN
96 (Top) THS; (Bottom) ILN
97 (Top) ILN; (Bottom) Corbis
98 IFE/IAO

99 (Top) Barbara Kharouf Collection; (Bottom) Don Lynch
100–101 IFE/IAO
102–103 IFE/IAO
104 (Top) BB; (Bottom) *Cork Examiner*
105 THS

Chapter Five
106–107 IFE/IAO
108 BB
109 (Top) Maritime Museum of the Atlantic; (Middle) NSARM; (Bottom) NSARM
110 (Top) NG
110 (Bottom) WHOI
111 WHOI
112 (Top) Anita Brosius, courtesy of the Lamont-Doherty Geological Observatory; (Bottom) MPC
113 (Top) Naval Historical Center; (Bottom) Emory Kristof © NG
114 (Top) Robert Ballard/WHOI; (Bottom) Emory Kristof © NG
115 Emory Kristof © NG
116 Robert Ballard/WHOI
116–117 IFE/IAO
118 Robert Ballard and Martin Bowen/WHOI
119 Both photos Perry Thorsvik © NG
120–121 IFE/IAO
121 Photo from *Ghosts of the Abyss* courtesy of Walden Media. Copyright © 2003 by Walden Media, LLC. All rights reserved.
122–123 IFE/IAO

Chapter Six
126–127 Mosaic created by Hanumant Singh, WHOI/URI-GSO/@IFE: The images that make up this mosaic were taken by the *Hercules* ROV during an expedition lead by Dr. Robert D. Ballard.
All other photos IFE/IAO

Chapter Seven
All photos IFE/IAO

INDEX

INDEX *(cont'd)*

SELECTED BIBLIOGRAPHY

Books

Ballard Robert D. and Rick Archbold. *Lost Liners*. New York: Hyperion, 1997.

Ballard, Robert D. *The Discovery of the* Titanic. New York: Warner Books, 1987.

Ballard, Robert D., with Michael Sweeney. *Return to* Titanic: *A New Look at the World's Most Famous Ship*. Washington D.C.: *National Geographic*, 2004.

Beesley, Lawrence. *The Loss of S.S. Titanic: Its Story and its Lessons*. Boston: Houghton Mifflin Co., 2000.

Biel, Steven. *Down with the Old Canoe: A Cultural History of the* Titanic *Disaster*. New York: W.W. Norton & Co., 1996.

Bonsall, Thomas E. Titanic: *The Story of the Great White Star Trio: The* Olympic, *the* Titanic *and the* Britannic. New York: Gallery Books, 1987.

Brewster, Hugh and Laurie Coulter. *882 1/2 Amazing Answers to your Questions about the* Titanic. New York: Scholastic Books, 1998.

Brown, David G. *The Last Log of the* Titanic. Camden ME: International Marine, 2000.

Brown, Richard. *Voyage of the Iceberg: The Story of the Iceberg that Sank the* Titanic. Toronto: Lorimer, 1983.

Davie, Michael. Titanic: *The Death and Life of a Legend*. New York: Alfred A. Knopf, 1987.

Dudman, John. *The Sinking of the* Titanic. Hove: Wayland, 1987.

Eaton, John P. and Charles A. Haas. Titanic: *Destination Disaster: The Legends and the Reality*. New York: Norton, 1996.

Eaton, John P. and Charles A. Haas. Titanic: *Triumph and Tragedy*. New York and London: W.W. Norton and Co., 1986.

Gardiner, Robin, and Dan van der Vat. *The* Titanic *Conspiracy*. New York: Carol Publishing Group, 1996.

Gracie Archibald. Titanic: *A Survivor's Story*. Chicago: Academy Chicago Publishers, 1998.

Hyslop, David, Alastair Forsyth, and Sheila Jemima. Photos by John Lawrence. Titanic *Voices: Memories of the Fateful Voyage*. New York: St. Martin's Press, 1997.

Jessop, Violet. Titanic *Survivor: The Newly Discovered Memoirs of Violet Jessop, who Survived Both the* Titanic *and* Britannic *Disasters*. Dobbs Ferry, NY: Sheridan House, 1997.

Lord, Walter. *A Night to Remember*. New York: Henry Holt and Company, 1955.

Lord, Walter. *The Night Lives On: The Untold Stories & Secrets Behind the Sinking of the Unsinkable Ship –* Titanic. New York: Morrow, 1986.

Lynch, Don. Titanic: *An Illustrated History*. New York, Hyperion, 1992.

McCluskie, Tom. *Anatomy of the* Titanic. San Diego: Thunder Bay Press, 1998.

McMillan, Beverly, Stanley Lehrer, and the staff of the Mariners' Museum. Titanic: *Fortune and Fate: Letters, Mementos, and Personal Effects from Those Who Sailed on the Lost Ship*. New York: Simon & Schuster; Newport News, Va.: Mariner's Museum, 1998.

O'Donnell, E. E. *The Last Days of the* Titanic: *Photographs and Mementos of the Tragic Maiden Voyage*. Niwot, Colo.: Roberts Rinehart Publishers, 1997.

Pellegrino, Charles R. *Ghosts of the* Titanic. New York: William Morrow, 2001.

Shapiro, Marc. *Total* Titanic: *The Most Up-To-Date Guide to the Disaster of the Century*. New York: Byron Preiss Multimedia; Pocket Books, 1998.

Wels, Susan. Titanic: *Legacy of the World's Greatest Ocean Liner*. Alexandria, Va.: Time-Life Books, 1997.

Articles

Ballard, Robert D. "Why is *Titanic* Vanishing?" *National Geographic* 206.6 (December 2004) p. 96-112

Broad, William J. "Scientists Warn That Visitors Are Loving *Titanic* to Death," *New York Times* August 9, 2003 Section A, page 1, column 1

Delgado, James P. "Diving on the *Titanic*." *Archaeology* January-February 2001, page unknown

MacInnis, Joe. "Live from the Bottom of the Sea." *Maclean's* July 08, 2005, p. 78

Schrope, Mark. "Welcome to Museum *Titanic* (Please Don't Touch)" *Popular Science* 267.1 (July 1, 2005) p. 49-55

Websites

Encyclopedia Titanica. HYPERLINK "http://www.encyclopedia-titanica.org/" http://www.encyclopedia-titanica.org/. Excellent one-stop source for *Titanic* facts.

Titanic Historical Society HYPERLINK "http://www.titanic1.org" www.titanic1.org. Official site of the first and arguably still the finest organization for *Titanic* enthusiasts.

WITH THANKS

I'd like to thank my fantastic team who worked so hard at sea to get these incredible images of *Titanic*, and Jared Ford for sorting through hours of high definition footage to find the true gems.

— *Robert Ballard*

To my wife, Catharine Lyons-King, for her incredible support during my work on this project.

—*Ian Coutts*

MADISON PRESS BOOKS would like to thank the following people for their help and expertise in creating this book: Dwight F. Coleman, PhD., Karen Kamuda of the THS, and LT. Jeremy B. Weirich, NOAA.

Project Editors: Ian Coutts, Anna Stancer

Editor: Blake Sproule

Book Design: Linda Gustafson, Counterpunch Inc.

Copyeditor: Jennifer Stokes

Index: Wendy Thomas

Color Separation, Proofing, Printing and Binding:
Oceanic Graphic Printing (China)

Produced by Madison Press Books

Diana Sullada, Art Director

Sandra L. Hall, Production Manager
Susan Barrable, Vice President, Finance and Production

Alison Maclean, Associate Publisher
Oliver Salzmann, President and Publisher